COMING OF AGE IN ANTHROPOLOGY

COMING OF AGE IN ANTHROPOLOGY

Commentaries on Growing Up
In the Global Village

Pamela J Peck

Peck, Pamela J (Pamela Janice)
    COMING OF AGE IN ANTHROPOLOGY
    Commentaries on Growing Up in the Global Village

1. Culture   2. Anthropology
3. Religion   4. Development Aid
5. Native Affairs   6. Ethnic Relations
7. Canada   8. Education

Printed in the United States of America.

ISBN: 978-1-4269-4820-6 (sc)
ISBN: 978-1-4269-4821-3 (e)

Trafford rev. 07/27/2011

 www.trafford.com

North America & International
toll-free: 1 888 232 4444 (USA & Canada)
phone: 250 383 6864 • fax: 812 355 4082

To the soul of humankind

Anyone who has begun to think places some portion of the world in jeopardy.

— John Dewey

PREFACE

In the early twentieth century, when Anthropology was still in its infancy, anthropologist Margaret Mead ventured into Polynesia and wrote a seminal book called **Coming of Age in Samoa**, followed shortly thereafter by a second ethnography called **Growing Up in New Guinea**. At the time, fieldwork studies that reported on these relatively isolated communities added greatly to our knowledge of the little known and even less understood so-called "primitive" cultures. Taken together, they allowed us to formulate new theories about culture and to test out our ideas about human society.

We are now in the early twenty-first century, and Anthropology is faced with a new reality. The world has evolved from a myriad of diverse and isolated villages into a single global community. And while it continues to be useful to know about the parts, the pressing concern for the discipline at this stage is how the parts relate to the whole. That is the focus of the present collection of commentaries.

Both the title **Coming of Age in Anthropology** and subtitle **Commentaries on Growing Up in the Global Village** borrow from the titles of Dr. Mead's original works. The similarity is intentional, and more than a simple play on words. For in less than a century, the world has transformed from a globe of villages to a global village. Whereas before it seemed we could go about our lives without undue concern for people on the other side of the planet, we are now forced to recognize that what we do in one part of the world affects every other part. We are one interrelated and interdependent social system.

It is time to "come of age" in—and to—this new global reality, and Anthropology, as the study of humankind, is particularly well positioned to serve as the principal vehicle for achieving this challenging task. Anthropology offers a framework for critically examining our economic, political and ideological institutions so that we might better decide how to have a world. The choice is clear: either we learn to "grow up" together, or we do not get to grow up at all.

Twenty commentaries are offered to this end, selected from a series of lectures, television interviews, retrospectives and informal talks I have offered to various audiences over a period spanning three decades—from 1980 to 2010—beginning with "Am I an Anthropologist Yet?", a reflection on what it means to be an anthropologist. From that starting point, the subject matter mirrors the familiar anthropological categories Margaret Mead included in her seminal work: family relationships, community life, education, religion, and the role of the dance.

But in the present case, those familiar categories take on new meaning and reach into new dimensions. The family is the human family, all seven billion of us, and the commentaries, like "Positive Prejudice" and "Booked for Lunch", focus on our ethnic relations. The community is the global community—the global village—and I have included a number of talks, such as "Sit and Sing—and Surrender to God" about cross-cultural understanding and development aid. Education, like "May a Little Child Lead You" and "A Four-Letter Word" is about the need for global education. Religion looks at the clash of ideologies and religious fundamentalism as well as the essential unity of all religions, and the most lengthy article—perhaps deservedly so—"Missing and Presumed Dead" falls in this category; it is a lecture I presented on the infamous and deadly terrorist attack of "nine-eleven". The role of the dance is the movement of our national and international life. Included here are talks about cultural phenomena such as world expositions and Olympic games, large-scale events that engender worldwide attention and have global significance. I have also directed attention to my own native land, reflecting on our socio-cultural institutions, the treatment of Canada's indigenous peoples and the so-called Canadian unity crisis. In spite of the wide variety of subject matter, the goal is singular: to foster and enhance cross-cultural understanding in order that we may together create a more peaceful world.

While Margaret Mead inspired the title and subtitle of the present volume, I am indebted to many good minds for the ideas expressed in the various commentaries. Among those writers who must be named are preeminent figures like Karl Marx and C.G. Jung, along with Fritjof Capra, Eric Fromm and Paul Ricoeur. I would especially like to add the names of Martin Buber, Karen Armstrong and Ken Wilber. Anyone familiar with the works of the above will recognize my indebtedness to these outstanding thinkers. I would be remiss by not also including the many people in the various educational and development agencies who have invited me to be a part of their world; I have gained a great deal by my associations with them. And finally, I want to express my deepest thanks to Ken Johnson, editor, partner and best friend, whose sustained support in every way has allowed me the privilege of writing and publishing this volume and many other creative works.

THE COMMENTARIES

AM I AN ANTHROPOLOGIST YET?

Addendum to the PhD Dissertation
University of British Columbia, 1980

I have often heard anthropologists who are seasoned in the profession speak about fieldwork as a rite of passage. It is only fitting, perhaps, that they characterize the experience in a language peculiar to their own discipline, a kind of colloquial reference to a deemed requirement for admitting others into their fraternity. The serious student of Anthropology soon learns that s/he must endure the ritual, entering abruptly and fully into its mystique without a clear set of instructions that would ensure safe passage. Somehow the correct procedure cannot be communicated in advance; the experience itself is the essential ingredient in the making of an anthropologist. Most look forward to it, eager to gloss over the theory and get on with it, no longer content to realize the ethnography through someone else's account.

While the necessity to do fieldwork is spelled out clearly enough, precisely what is to happen to the candidate in the field has been less well articulated. When newly emerged initiates write about the fieldwork experience—and some leave out the account entirely—it can read a bit like the proverbial "How I Spent My Summer Vacation". The kind and degree of adjustment to and accommodation by the indigenous culture, and how one went about doing what it is one does in the field would seem to be what should be delivered up. As time sharpens critical understanding and begs deeper shades of honesty, a more rounded account ought to be expected—a tale of the good, the bad and the ugly, as it were.

Living in another culture, learning the language, coming to think in local categories, discovering the relationship between economy, polity and ideology—there is something in all of this, to be sure. It is a part of what it takes to make an anthropologist. But it is not yet the rite.

A rite of passage entails separation, transition and reintegration. The point of the comparison is that it is not only what the initiate moves to that is significant but also what s/he is separated from. To separate oneself from the home environment for a time in order to intellectualize an alternative system of meaning is to remove oneself from one's own sources of truth. It is a self-imposed alienation, a psychological condition of what loneliness entails. Transition combines discomfort and illumination in an uneasy partnership, and the process, which gradually defines the constructs of another and different people, inevitably enlightens the initiate to knowledge that one's own culture cannot be accepted on its own terms. Reintegration settles on what is irrevocably cultural about the self, and with the new awareness, the anthropologist emerges to see the familiar anew. Coming to terms with the cultural self: that is the rite. In the words of St. Paul, "For now we see through a glass, darkly; but then face-to-face: now I know in part; but then I shall know even as also I am known" (I Corinthians 13:12).

I spent the greater part of two years doing fieldwork, the bulk of that time in a small village on an outer island in Fiji. While there I lived in a traditional thatched hut that I paid to have built for me. It was lovely, a masterpiece of local artistry which one day not too distant will be reminiscent of another age; I count myself one of the last to be able to do fieldwork in so natural and aesthetic a habitat. I sustained myself on the local diet—yams, taro, cassava and fish, with pork or beef a welcome addition on special holidays and ceremonial occasions; I liked the food. I took part in village life and felt from the beginning, a warmth and love for the place and the people. And I set about to learn the language, and although I did not achieve the degree of fluency I had hoped to enjoy, I came to think in local categories. As time progressed, the meanings deepened and the effort paid off. Understanding the language is a necessity for good fieldwork.

All this seems to be what anthropologists do. But for me it could not count as the decisive ritual. Before working in Fiji, I had visited more than thirty foreign countries and lived for a time in some of them, and Fijian was the seventh foreign language I was learning. What was decisive, however, in the making of the anthropologist was my encounter with the European culture through the eyes of the outsider. For not only did I see European thought-ways juxtaposed with the activities and ideas of another and different people but I came face to face with the cultural relativity of a universal model of the moral man. I saw it in people like the General Secretary of the YMCA of New Zealand, laboring now in Western Samoa to establish a YMCA in that Pacific island nation. He was (mistakenly) able to perceive development as somehow culturally neutral. I saw it again in people from the Canadian International Development Agency whose office towers spill across the Ottawa River into Hull, Quebec. These people in the Non-Governmental Organization Division are convinced of the worth of what they do. I admire these dedicated Europeans. Yet, instructed as I am to step outside my categories, I am forced to see the cultural signature on the programs they fashion. It challenges me to know how an anthropologist is to be responsible in a world community. Is there a starting-point or an ending-point in determining what is irrevocably cultural about the self?

Or is it too late to consider these questions in a world approaching the 21st century in the midst of a communication revolution? It is said that fools rush in where angels fear to tread. That may be so. But angels are too remote to guide the process of change in today's international community. There may well be more wisdom to the adage, "No fools, no fun!".

SIT AND SING—AND SURRENDER TO GOD

Talk given to World Development Staff and Volunteers,
YMCA of Vancouver, 1981

I'm going to talk for the next few minutes about evaluating foreign aid programs in general and about the YMCA project in particular. But I'm going to introduce it in a rather oblique fashion in order to focus on what I think is a very critical factor in the success of these aid programs.

Someone once asked Baba Hari Das, a Hindu mystic, what we should do to save the planet. His answer was this: "Sit and sing—and surrender to God."

This is clearly an eastern worldview and one to which we do not readily subscribe, because to sit while people starve does not sit well with us. And sing? You've heard those wailing sounds the Ethiopians make each morning as they bury their dead; we cannot sing to that tune. As for surrender, when survival of the planet is at stake we don't surrender to anything!

Now this is not to diminish Hindu philosophy. There is a great deal of wisdom contained in those few words from the Hindu saint. It is based on a philosophy of dispassion—something quite outside our cultural reference. It serves to remind us that the assumptions we bring to a cross-cultural encounter are not necessarily accepted or even understood. And almost all the programs of the NGO community in Canada operate in the cross-cultural setting. We invest time, human energy, knowledge, skills, technology—and a great deal of money—and we don't want our projects to fail. But too often they do fail—and for the wrong reason.

Let me give you a couple of examples before we consider the Fiji project. Back in the 60's, when Micronesia was the US Trust Territory of the Pacific Islands under UN authority, the United States Department of the Interior sent a number of community development officers (CDO's) into the region. The thing that really got to them was the prevalence of flies, so one of the CDO's determined to get rid of them. He got the village headman to bring the people together so he could lecture them about the health hazards of these little insects. And just to make sure they were clear on what he was talking about, he used a poster size picture of a fly and displayed it as he delivered his talk.

The CDO told the villagers about how flies breed, about how they spread disease and about how to break the parasite cycle by destroying their breeding grounds. The villagers listened politely and when the lecture was over, they quietly got up and walked away. The CDO was puzzled, and he said to the headman who had organized the meeting, "Why didn't they respond? What did I do wrong?" The headman replied, "Well, you see, we're not really concerned about this. And now I see why you state-siders—(that's what they called the Americans down there)—now I see why you state-siders get so upset about flies." Then, placing his thumb and index finger a quarter-inch apart, he continued, "But down here, they're only this big."

A couple of weeks ago I had a meeting with a Canadian engineer working in Nepal. They are sinking some wells in a valley just south of Kathmandu. And he was saying, "You know, I really like this work; it's really worth doing. And it gives me a real sense of satisfaction. But it's so frustrating. Because unless I'm right there, doing the work with them, nothing gets done. If I leave Nepal and come to Canada for six months, when I return, nothing has happened since the day I left."

Well, the first obvious question is, do they want the wells? "Oh, yes," he says, "they want them and they need them." So I say, "For goodness sake, people have lived in that valley for hundreds and hundreds of years. And they have survived—and that's a very harsh environment. That means they've got some kind of blueprint for survival. (He was an engineer so I talked about blueprints.) So in order to work their blueprint, they must have some form of social organization, some political structure they've worked out in order to get things done. And if you could know what that is and plug into it, then they would build those wells by themselves. And you could do what you are supposed to do—be a technical adviser. For example, I know those villages have panchayats. A panchayat is a local village council usually composed of five men. ('Panch' is the Hindi word for 'five'.) It's the duty of those men to see to these kinds of things. What they lack is technology and resources—but they've got the required human energy. It just needs to be unleashed.

Now, let's look at the Fiji project and see why it is working so well. What did we find out when we evaluated it? Well, we found out that the YMCA introduced a project based on unrestricted exchange—that's the buying and selling of goods and services with money—into an economy based on continuing prescribed exchange. That's the ongoing exchange of goods and services and ceremonial valuables between real and imagined kinship groups, that is, groups related through blood or marriage or through political alliance.

And we found out that the YMCA introduced a project based on participatory democracy—that's the setting up of committee structures with duly elected leaders and an open decision-making process—into a society based on patriarchal authority. That's a chieftainship where a few people at the top talk and give out orders and the many people beneath them listen and carry out those orders.

Now, that project shouldn't have worked at all! It should have fallen on its face. But it didn't—because of one critical factor. I'm calling it cultural brokerage. You see, the YMCA staff person who set it all up went and lived for a number of years in Fiji. Now that's a luxury few NGO's can afford. But what that experience did was make that man realize that while the goals and objectives were agreed, the cultural referents were not. He knew he couldn't go into those villages and make things happen. People might have worked alongside him so long as he was there—the Fijians are very polite—but once he left, chances are everything would grind to at halt. Like in Nepal. So what he did instead was take a number of young men from these villages and train them in the philosophy of community development.

He made sure the goals were clear and agreed upon, and then he set them loose back in the villages. These young men knew how to plug the projects into the existing social institutions and unleash that human energy. But something else happened too: in the process, those very social institutions were gradually modified and transformed.

That's the difference. And that's good because we're not in the business of preserving cultures . . . of making sure things don't change. People and cultures are changing all the time. We often hear the old adage that people resist change. People don't resist change; they just resist change that doesn't make sense to them.

So the lesson is this: when we invest human energy, knowledge, skills, technology and time—not to mention a great deal of money—we don't want our projects to fail. So we have a tendency to go in there and do it ourselves. And when we do that, the projects do fail. And sometimes they fail because of something that is only as big as a fly. If instead we can figure out what things turn on, culturally speaking, and plug the project into that, well then, we can sit and sing—and surrender to God. And the planet will save itself.

MISSIONARIES NEVER DIE

Talk given to the Metropolitan Board of Governors
Vancouver YMCA, on the occasion of the Presentation of the
Dissertation **Missionary Analogues**, October 1982

I have a little book here that I would like to give to the Director of your International Development Committee and, through him, to all of you. It's called "Missionary Analogues" and it is a description of the Rural Work Program of the YMCA of Fiji. And that development program is possible in large part because of the people right here in this room. You see that the book looks rather big. There is a custom in Fiji that when you give someone something and it looks big, you have to say that it's just little. Like the tabua, the whale's tooth. It's the highest form of traditional wealth in Fiji. When one chief wants to give a tabua to another chief, he'll say, "Here's a little batina." Batina means "tooth"; he won't even say that it's a tabua.

Well, that's not the reason I say this is just a little book. I say it's little because when you look inside, you see that there is script on only one side of the page. And it's double-spaced.

And it has wide margins. That's because it has been written in the formal style of a dissertation. If it were written up like an ordinary book, it would probably be so small that you could slip it in your pocket alongside your calculator!

Well, the reason I'm telling you this is because when you get past the formality of the presentation, you will discover a story. And the story is being told by the Fijians—and they're good storytellers. Sometimes the story is sad, because like for all of us, some of the things that happen to them are not happy things. And sometimes it's funny. Because, you know, life should not be taken too seriously. For example, did you know that for a while some people in Fiji thought that YMCA stood for Young Men's Cabbage Association? That's because one of the first things the new YMCA clubs used to do was plant cabbage.

Well, I was saying that the Fijians are telling their story. And the story goes something like this. For a long time we were living in our traditional Fijian way of life and it served us well. Meanwhile, the outside world was changing. And the people—the Europeans—they were changing too, in order to keep pace with the changing world. But we were pretty much cut off from the outside world and we didn't even know it was changing. And then all of a sudden the change caught up with us and we didn't know what to do about it. We knew that we would have to change. But we didn't know the way. And then, seemingly out of nowhere came these Europeans, the YMCA, and they said, "We have come to show you the way". And in the book the Fijians are saying, you know, it's funny, because this happened to us once before. It was over a century ago. We were living in isolated tribes and we were afraid of each other. And when we came in contact, we used to kill each other. And to show you the depravity of that kind of life, after we did the killing, we used to eat each other. (And Fiji is famous for its cannibalism.) Into that darkness, seemingly out of nowhere came these Europeans, the missionaries, and they said, "We have come to show you the way." That's where the title "Missionary Analogues" comes from. This dissertation is to be published as a monograph, and I'm thinking to call it "Missionaries Never Die". Because they don't, you see.

So the Fijians are telling their story in this book. And I am presenting the book on behalf of them. I also want to present it on behalf of your International Development staff. Now what should I say about them? Well, when I was trying to decide what was the most important thing to tell you today, I was thinking back to how I came to do this research in the first place. It was only then that I realized that they had talked me into it! Well, they are good friends and they helped me a lot. They set it all up, wrote all the letters and got all the file material for me and got me going. And they keep me involved in the Y. Whenever the Fijians come to Canada or any of the Vancouver people go to Fiji, they always invite me to meet and talk with them.

There's one other group I want to present this book on behalf of and that is the International Development Research Centre in Ottawa. They're the ones who funded this research. They wanted this kind of study to be done because they are beginning to realize that if development is to be done in human terms, it's going to have to be done by people like you. Governments can't do it. And it's not happening in our bilateral or multilateral aid programs, or through the World Bank or by private industry. No, it has to be done by the people in the voluntary agencies. It's not that these other people are not capable, but they have neither the skill nor the will to do development in human terms.

Now we are just an ordinary group of people. But what distinguishes us is that we have a conviction about how to have a world. And in the YMCA, that conviction includes the idea that when you meet someone, you have to meet the whole person. And that's the only sane way to go about doing anything, because this is a very dangerous world. We are making more and bigger instruments of death, and they're all in place, just waiting for us. And do you know what they are waiting for? They're waiting for us to become just a little bit more insane. But development in human terms does not allow for that kind of insanity. So I hope you will accept this book as a symbol of what you are about. And I hope you will get solidly behind your international development program and, like they say, go for it!

GETTING TO KNOW YOU

Talk given to the Board of Governors, YMCA of Fiji,
on the Presentation of the Dissertation
Missionary Analogues. November, 1982

I think most of you know that a few years ago I came to Fiji to study your YMCA Rural Work program. I spent most of my time on Ngau Island; I also spent some time in Ra. I came here to your national office to work with the Rural Work Director and the General Secretary. Then I went to Western Samoa to talk with the General Secretary of the YMCA of New Zealand who introduced the program here in Fiji. And then I returned to Canada to talk with the people in the YMCA of Vancouver, and to Ottawa to talk with the people at CIDA, the Canadian International Development Agency.

Now why go to all that bother? Why make such a long journey? Well, as I see it, a journey has two parts to it. There is the outer journey, the traveling from place to place to meet and talk with people. And there is the inner journey, the traveling that goes on in the mind. And that inner journey is always tied up with a question to be answered, something that you have to understand. And for me, I wasn't just interested in knowing about rural development in Fiji; I wanted to understand that whole relationship between Europeans and Fijians through something called a YMCA.

That was the journey — and the journey led to a discovery. The discovery is this: what we development people are doing in Fiji today through agencies like the YMCA is an awful lot like what the missionaries did here well over a century ago. That's where the title "Missionary Analogues" comes from. An analogue is something that is like something else. Development is like Christianity.

It's difficult to see at first because we have to put a whole new language around it. For example, we don't talk about Christian charity anymore, but we bring in our foreign aid. Both of those things are about money that has some expectation tied to it. We don't come in and build a church, but we do set up an agency. And the organization of the agency is a lot like the organization of a church, with committees, budgets, annual meetings and all that. And we don't talk about converting people anymore, but we do talk about being in charge of our own lives. Like conversion, that process, which we call individuation, is about being changed, about being a new kind of person.

Well, the point of discovering all this is that we Europeans have got to understand what it is we are asking you Fijians to do and to be. We don't see it because it's our culture, and we don't see our culture because we live inside of it. For your part, I think it's important that you understand European culture and the way Europeans think. Because it's really different from na i tovo vakaviti ("the Fijian way of life"), and now this European way of life is becoming part of na i tovo vakaviti.

It's all very confusing. If you don't understand it you can't know yourself. And if you don't know yourself you can't take care of yourself. And if you can't take care of yourself, you can't take care of other people. And the whole thing breaks down.

So this is your copy of the journey. The Canadians have their copy and it is their chance to better understand you. This is your opportunity to better know us. So I hope it will have meaning for you and that it will help all of us to more perfectly love one another.

THE BEARERS OF THE MESSAGE

Talk given to the Women's Discussion Group
Methodist Church of Fiji. Suva, 1983

I want to begin by saying that I am really happy to be here with you because I think it is a very important thing that you have been called to do. You might not think that I feel this way when you hear me talk because I am not going to glorify either the Church or the development agencies. But I think it would be helpful for you to bear in mind that I make a very clear distinction between the Church as an institution of organized religion and human beings as believing Christians.

Now I have some notes here, but I'm not planning to use them in a formal way. I brought them along in case I forget what I want to say. So I'm thinking to put out some ideas for about fifteen or twenty minutes and then let you comment or ask questions or even reject what I say. And I want you to know that I won't be upset if you do reject my ideas, because I have never felt it very honest or in any way useful to say what I think people want to hear. On the other hand, it is diplomatic—but I'm not a diplomat.

I want to tell you a story.

Somewhere around the close of the 19th century or the beginning of the 20th—I don't remember the exact year and it doesn't matter—there was a child born in the city of Madras in south India. Being born into a Hindu family, his parents did what many Hindu parents do: they consulted an astrologer to find out about this new soul in their midst. The astrologer told them that this child, whose name was Krishnamurti, had a very favorable aura and that he would grow up to be a very spiritual person. In that his parents were Brahmin Hindus, I'm sure they were very pleased.

Also in Madras at this time was the headquarters of the Theosophical Society of India, which was and is a quasi-religious organization investigating psychic phenomena and the occult. From their own psychic insights, they determined there would be born in their midst a new world teacher. When they heard about Krishnamurti, they went to his father and asked permission to take the child and educate him for this important role. The father agreed, so they took Krishnamurti and prepared him to be the new world teacher of the Theosophical Society. But when the young man matured, he rejected both the role and the organization which it represented and set about to speak the truth as he understood it to be. That's important: he removed himself from the whole system of socialization in which he was reared. And it is probably because of that move that he became a truly remarkable educator. The point, of course, is that in order to find yourself you have to first lose yourself.

One day a young man asked Krishnamurti this question: "Do you think that Untouchables should be allowed in the temples?" Krishnamurti replied, "Well, there should be no temples." Now, he was not attacking Hinduism as some kind of heathen religion. He himself was a Brahmin Hindu and in the course of his education, he became well acquainted with the Vedic literature. What he was saying to the inquirer is this: young man, your question pales with insignificance when you consider the wider question as to how a five-thousand-year-old tradition of Hindu philosophy could be reduced to such a narrow system of religious conformity.

That is my story. Now I would like to tell you another one. This one is a children's story, and children's stories usually contain great wisdom because children are not easily fooled. And the reason they are not easily fooled is because they are not yet fully socialized. Their minds usually reflect a remarkable clarity.

This story is called "The Emperor's New Clothes" and some of you may have heard it. It is about an emperor who felt it either his privilege or his obligation to be dressed finer than anyone else in the kingdom. (There's a fair bit of this going on in England at the present time.) So anyway, the emperor kept instructing his clothiers to weave him finer and still finer cloth. Perhaps it was out of desperation that they finally decided to weave him a cloth so fine that you could neither see nor feel it. In other words, the cloth would not really be there. Because if it were there, it wouldn't be fine enough, you see. So they set up the looms and they began to weave the imaginary cloth. They summoned the emperor to witness the marvel: cloth so fine that you could neither see nor feel it. The emperor was thrilled. "It's the finest cloth in the kingdom," he proclaimed. Perhaps because the emperor believed it, the clothiers themselves began to believe it, and soon word spread around the kingdom about the emperor's new clothes. When the weaving was finished, they removed the cloth from the loom, and they cut and stitched it into a fine garment.

Finally the day arrived for the emperor to show his new clothes. People gathered in the streets around the palace. Then the emperor appeared, dressed in his new attire. The people exclaimed, "Ah, the emperor's new clothes, how fine and lovely they are!" And then a child, who did not see through a glass dimly, said, "But he's not wearing any clothes!" (Boy, if you want to enter the Kingdom, you had better come as a child.) And when they heard the words of the child, the people saw through the deception and they cried after him, "He's not wearing any clothes! The emperor has no clothes!" (And a little child led them.)

That's my second story. Now what these two stories have in common is that they are both about something that I am going to call false consciousness. The first one—about the temples—structures of the physical world, built for the spiritual life of a people, which excludes some of those same people. The second one—about the clothes—structures of the mind designed to convince people that things exist when they don't really exist. I am going to talk about false consciousness in relation to the two institutions of the Western world concerned with the spiritual life of people: Christianity, and its secular counterpart, world development.

Now the central image of the spiritual life is journey. Each of us is on a journey. That's what life is. And we are here, incidentally, companions on that journey. A journey has two parts: the outer journey—that moving about from place to place in the physical world, and the inner journey—that traveling that goes on in our minds. Taken together, these two facets of journey constitute our experience of the knowable world. In short, it is our consciousness.

The human journey seems to have started out okay. It certainly began in the perfect place to begin a journey: a beautiful garden, so the myth says, with fruit trees, flowing water and clean air. Probably a nuclear free zone. Anyway, everything we wish we still had today. Everything there was life giving. And then there were those two symbols of human life giving: the male and the female. Now the really incredible thing about all this is that there should have been anything happening at all. Just think of it: how could it have possibly come into being! Take any particular facet of it, like a papaya, for example. What could possibly be the recipe for a papaya! An average size one must have about a cup and a half of water but after that I'm stuck. I know it also contains Vitamin A and Vitamin C and digestive enzymes but I have no idea what they are made of. Or take the banana: have you ever noticed that the skin of every banana fits perfectly! And oranges, how they come wrapped up in little sections like that. Sort of gourmet packaging. That's one thing you've got to say for God: She sure can cook! Well, anyway, these two people were there, having all of this, and the whole point was just to be there—the outer journey—and to contemplate being there—the inner journey. In short, life was a joyful play of consciousness.

And then something went wrong. Those two bearers of consciousness went out and developed a false consciousness. Now it doesn't say in Genesis that they developed a false consciousness. What it says is that they ate from the tree of knowledge of good and evil. But just think about that for a moment. What does it mean to take inside yourself knowledge of good and evil? It means that from that point onward, some things are good and other things are bad, some things are right and other things are wrong, some things are high and other things are low. That last one is mainly for people: it's Her Royal Highness and my common lowness. In other words, they learned to discriminate—and that spelled the beginning of human society. Because, you see, in nature there are no discriminations. Things are not good or bad, right or wrong; they just are—and everything is connected to everything else. Nature is a unified whole. That's why they became aware of and embarrassed about their nakedness. Because they separated themselves from the essential unity of things and saw themselves as separate egos. They became, as it were, a people in need of atonement—at-one-ment. And the history of human society is the history of a race of people in need of atonement. So they transformed nature into culture and consciousness into false consciousness. In other words, they began the human journey but they got lost.

Well, when you are on a journey and you get lost, you need someone to come and show you the way. And someone did come and He said, "I am the way to take the human journey. Come and follow me." And we are all familiar with the story. But mind you, by the time Jesus did come and do his thing, that false consciousness had manifested itself in some deeply entrenched social institutions. Institutions with rules and roles, rights, duties and obligations, well established patterns for the distribution of wealth and power. People were pretty agreed about who was in control of things and who owned the earth. So when you have someone coming along and saying that the meek are going to inherit the earth, you've got big trouble. Because in order for the meek to inherit the earth, there are a lot of things that are going to have to be turned upside down. I mean, just take a look around you. You know the people who are inheriting the earth—and they are not meek people! So when someone is saying the unsayable, you have to get rid of him. Go nail him to a tree somewhere. And, of course, that's what they did.

Well, the Christian community is the bearer of that message and it had better keep it alive. But it has to do so at tremendous odds. Because when we look at the history of Christianity, it's not a pretty picture! Union of church and state, holy wars, holy empires. The Church has at times and in places been more concerned to be a structure to perpetuate the status quo than to be a movement that liberates people from it. Take the Church of England, for example. In England, the Church still literally crowns the monarch. And monarchy represents one of the cleverest deceptions and one of the most inequitable social systems in the history of human society: the feudal state. The feudal state is based on there being a very small, very wealthy, titled, hereditary ruling class which owns the land and the resources, and a massive poor, landless class of workers. Now that's a pretty blatant example. But there are more subtle ones. Over the years, the Church has become the moral institution of society making decisions on everything from birth control to whether women should be allowed ordination. Think of that last one for a moment. Should women be allowed in the pulpit? Should Untouchables be allowed in the temples? Should Fijians be allowed in the Rotary Club? Missing the point!

Well, the redeeming factor in all of this is that there are the faithful, the bearers of the message. In spite of that, there are a lot of people who are saying good-bye to the Church. They just don't see it as the framework within which to take the human journey. But if they don't find it in the Church, they've got to find it somewhere. Because, like it or not, they are still on the human journey and this is no Garden of Eden! So where have they turned? Some have turned to Eastern religion—to transcendental meditation, Zen Buddhism, raja yoga, Krishna consciousness . . .. Others have turned to psychology—to psychotherapy, psychoanalysis, psychiatry— and others to mind-altering experiences such as hallucinogenic drugs. But probably the mainstream of those who have left the Church have headed into the voluntary agencies where there is a whole new emphasis on individual and community development. And it is the programs of these agencies that make up the new thrust in human development.

Like the early Christian communities, these agencies started out okay. But like the Church, they too are now becoming deeply entrenched social institutions. As such, they are becoming more agents of the status quo than agents of change. A lot of it has to do with their preoccupation with funding, the idea that if you just have enough money you can come up with the right program. Rather than the other way around, that if you are really meeting the needs of the people, the resources will come. Mother Teresa figured that one out, and Gandhi and a few others. So if your main concern is funding, you look to the people who've got the money. And who are they? Government and big business. So you end up running the kinds of programs that government and big business want run. And to make sure you are in good with them, you put the big people on your boards and committees, and you make the Queen or the Governor-General or whatever title is the top one the honorary president or chairman of the agency. And that's just about where we are today. Again, the redeeming factor in all of this is that there are still the faithful, the bearers of the message.

Well, it can be a bit depressing to think through all this and figure out what is happening, especially to the institutions you cherish. Sometimes it seems it would be a lot easier just to accept the illusion, to believe in the constructs, to see through a glass dimly, believing that when you die and get to the Kingdom then you will see face to face. But the Kingdom is here and now.

The Kingdom is within you. That is the message. So when you don't get the message, everybody loses. We go through life alienated, anxious, guilty, lonely and unrelated. We build up psychological defense systems to protect ourselves from each other. And then we project those psychological defenses into the physical world, nationally and internationally, until today we have defense systems so sophisticated on the planet that they threaten the very continuation of the human journey. And it all comes back to that one great big social taboo—the taboo against knowing who you are. Because if you know yourself, it threatens the social order. Everything has to be kept in order.

Living in nature, living in the here and now, requires a great deal of spontaneity. But we no longer know how to live spontaneously. We have forgotten the cosmic dance. We have forgotten that life is a joyful play of consciousness.

PEDAGOGY OF THE ELITE

Talk presented at a Conference on Education,
University of British Columbia, 1984

Does anything meaningful or useful come out of all this elitist research activity going on around our universities? Or, put another way, what, if any, is the practical value of "pure" research? That is the question we are to consider.

Well, let us examine a piece of "pure" research. And let's not bias the critique in our favour: let's look to a discipline that distinguishes itself for its elitism and its irrelevancy. Next to a subject like Latin, that discipline would have to be Anthropology. Now I don't mean those physical anthropologists or archaeologists who go about digging up things; they at least come up with something you can put your hands on. And, if you're lucky, you might, as a result of their digging around, find out where you really did come from. No, I'm talking about the social and cultural anthropologists, the ones who head off into the far corners of the earth, come back one or two years later and write a book about pointless rituals and mindless superstitions. And the ones who get hooked on things that really don't even happen anymore like human sacrifice, female infanticide, widow strangling, cannibalism: I'm talking about things, in short, that happened in 19th-century Fiji.

Well, let's take the case of Fiji. Have any of you seen the latest version of "Mutiny on the Bounty"? There's a scene in there after the mutiny, where Captain Bligh is in his little boat, with his little crew, and their little stores, all three running very low, and he's deciding what to do next. They've already stopped at the island of Tofua and they've had to make a quick getaway because the natives aren't very friendly.

There they are, sailing westward. They're tired, they're hungry, they're thirsty and they're suffering from exposure. And just off the horizon are 350 of the loveliest and most lush islands in the whole of the South Pacific: the Fiji Islands. Taro, breadfruit, coconuts, mangoes, papaya, fresh water and a reef full of fish: everything they need to sustain life. But Bligh says to his crew, "We can't stop there, because the people who inhabit those islands are the most savage in the whole of the South Pacific. What's more, they have perfected cannibalism into a science." A scene or two later, one of his mutinied crew is dying and that man says to Bligh, "When I'm dead, there's nothing here in this body that is me. It's just a chunk of flesh. Use that chunk of flesh to save these dying men." And Bligh replies, "No, no, we do not eat human flesh; we are civilized men, and civilized men we shall die."

There you have it: savage Fijians on the one hand and civilized Englishmen on the other. That parallel intrigues me because they're both members of the same species. Yet they have a very different idea of what it means to be human.

Well, I went to the Fiji Islands. In fact, I went to that same area where Bligh sailed on by. The water there is called the Bligh Strait; they named it after him. The closest island is called Ngau. And it's a lucky thing for him that he didn't stop there. Because that's the island in Fiji where cannibalism is said to have originated. Not only that, the cannibals on Ngau further distinguished themselves by cooking and serving the bokola whole. (Bokola is the name they gave to the bodies destined for the cannibal ovens.) They served the cooked bodies in one piece. You see, in other parts of Fiji, they would dismember the bodies, then cook and serve up the parts. And incidentally, they could cut up a human body with skill that would astonish a British surgeon. But on Ngau, they would put the whole body into the oven and when it was cooked, they would dress it up in feathers and finery, and then they would carry it in on a chair like they would a big chief. And then everybody would dig in. That was back in the nineteenth century.

As I was saying, I went to Ngau. I stayed there for two years and I came back and wrote a book. Then I went back to Fiji and stayed another year and now I'm writing another book. Pure research. Research about pointless rituals and mindless superstitions. I write about the old culture of Fiji with its human sacrifice and cannibalism, and about the coming of the missionaries with the Gospel of Christ to save the lost souls of the savages, and about the new missionaries, the development people, who are in there now, saving the Fijians all over again.

Now what's the point of knowing all of this? What on earth has that got to do with your life and with my life, right here and right now?

Well, it's got a lot to do with it. In fact, it's got everything to do with it. You see, the point is not that other people have pointless rituals and mindless superstitions. We think the things they do are pointless because we don't get the point. And we think the things they believe are mindless because we don't clue into their cultural mind. We know it's all in their heads, that it's just illusion. But it's real to them—and that makes all the difference in the world.

Now, what follows from that—and this is the point—is that we similarly respond to pointless rituals and mindless superstitions. We don't think the things we do are pointless because we see the point. And we don't think the things we believe are mindless because we know how to clue into this cultural mind. It's reality to us—and we play it for real. But it's not real at all; it's just illusion. And a very dangerous illusion at that, because it turns us into discriminating ego principles and that leads us to do all kinds of pointless and mindless things. Like building defense systems that are so powerful they will kill both them and us. It makes us see the world in opposites: things are good or bad, right or wrong, high or low. It's her Royal Highness and our common lowness. Who says so? Culture says so. Or more precisely, ideology says so. You and I have really had a number done on us. Why? Because there is an important relationship between ideology and domination. And the point of doing all this so-called pure research is to figure this out, to expose the process and to make ourselves the subject rather than the object of the event in order that we can decide how to have a world.

Now I speak from the point of view of Anthropology because that's my field. But you can take any piece of so-called "pure" research and put it to the test. Does it have anything to say about how to have a world. And incidentally, I don't think there is any such thing as pure research any more than I think there is a value-free science.

So let me first tell you how I think Anthropology might go about doing what it is capable of doing—and then let's take the case of Fiji and put it to the test. The point of doing research in Anthropology, in my mind, is to liberate the person from coercive illusions. Anthropology offers a process of critical reflection whereby one can see through the illusive constructs of culture, thereby freeing oneself, to the degree possible, from the constraints of the social world. In other words, the promise of Anthropology (and, in my mind, its greatest application) is the experience of emancipation by means of critical insight into relationships of power, the strength of which lies, in large part, in the fact that these relationships have not been seen through. So rather than generating mechanisms for justifying the organization of society—which so much of Anthropology is busy doing—the point is to free people from it. In this way, Anthropology is an emancipatory social science.

If you are familiar with Anthropology (or Sociology for that matter) you will immediately recognize the work of the critical theorists here. For those of you who are not, critical theory is a phenomenon of German intellectual history. Pure research! It is Marx's **Critique of Political Economy** that provides the paradigm, that work following in the intellectual tradition of Hegel's **Phenomenology of Mind** and paralleling the work of Freud and his theory of psychoanalysis. Pedagogy of the elite! It was Hegel who introduced the idea of liberation from coercive illusions through his analysis of the master-slave relationship. Marx offered a similar critique, this time directed to the economic world. And Freud contributed a new procedure of critical reflection, the idea here being that one operates, to a greater or lesser extent, from the illusive constructs of the unconscious. By seeing through the illusions and coming to terms with them, the sufferer can free himself. In other words, liberation from the illusive constraints of the inner world (Freud) finds its parallel in liberation from the illusive constraints of the outer world (Hegel), both of these lending themselves to a philosophical anthropology modeled on Marx's **Critique of Political Economy**. But here, you see, there is a shift from infrastructure to superstructure, from a critique of political economy to a critique of rationality. In other words, the point is to see through the illusive constructs of culture in order to get beyond ideology.

So now, let's go back to Fiji and to these two books about pointless rituals and mindless superstitions. You see, after people like Bligh returned to England with tales of human sacrifice and cannibalism, English missionaries headed out to Fiji to save the lost souls of the savages by converting them to Christianity. You can imagine what they went through, but they eventually succeeded. Today almost every Melanesian Fijian is a baptized Christian. So out went cannibalism—and out went a good deal of the traditional culture. Because, you see, you can't have one without the other. In went Christianity, and in went a good deal of the European culture. Because again, you can't have one without the other. And where Christianity left off with the notion of the one true God, development has picked up on a universal model of the moral man. So today in Fiji, we're finishing them off, culturally speaking. But that is not to say we are freeing them from the illusions of culture—we're just freeing them from the illusions of their culture and introducing them to the illusions of our own. Our task, in doing this research, then, is to reveal the process, to point out what is going on. And the reason for doing this is not only to be sensitive to what we are doing to other people but also to free ourselves from the very same illusions.

In the first book, **Missionary Analogues**, I outlined some parallels between the Christianization of Fiji more than a century ago and an international development program going on there right now. That investigation revealed that both the Christian mission and the development agency operate within the framework of the European socio-political system. The missionaries came with their charity—money—and set up missions in order to convert the Fijians. Now the development people come with their foreign aid and set up agencies in order to individuate the Fijians. It's the same process—only the language has changed. Charity and foreign aid: the shift from a system of continuing prescribed exchange—the exchange of valuables between real or designated kinship groups—to a system of unrestricted exchange—the buying and selling of goods and services with money. Mission and agency: the shift from a system of patriarchal authority—chieftainship—to a system of participatory democracy—shared leadership. And conversion and individuation: the shift from what I call institutionalized personality—which is akin to ascribed status—to institutionalized individuality—which is akin to achieved status.

Now, in the second book, called **In the Footsteps of the Missionaries**, I analyzed the journal of one of those young English missionaries in nineteenth century Fiji, and now that of a young Fijian community development worker in the twentieth century. Both the missionary and the development worker faced the same problems because they tried to operate within and between two sets of cultural categories in an attempt to do something (i.e., save people) that is in itself beyond culture. Neither of them, in the course of their assignments, was able to transcend the cultural idiom in order to truly "convert" the Fijians. Because, you see, both of them were trained to do what they did within the context of our European culture. This led me to look at what getting beyond culture is all about and that in turn led to the discovery of another analogue. The first one, you remember, was between Christianity and development; this second one is between Anthropology and Theology. And to see that latter analogue, I used the Marxist paradigm I outlined to you earlier.

Marx, of course, saw cultural illusion as a reflection of the class struggle. And in its positive aspect, he saw the possibility for an affirmation of man in revolution through a sociopolitical process. But Marx was a philosopher before he was a political economist and if we could recall the philosophy of the young Marx and align it with his later work in economics, we would be able to see that what is particularly valuable here is his art of interpretation applied to cultural structures. Hence, we are here involved in matching Marx's external critique of culture with a philosophical internal critique. And when we re-read Marx this way, we discover the hidden relation between ideology and domination. In his critique of religion, philosopher Paul Ricoeur says . . .

> This reading of ideology as a symptom of the phenomenon of domination will be the durable contribution of Marx beyond its political applications. From this point of view Marx does not solely belong to the Communists. Marxism, let it never be forgotten, appeared in Germany in the middle of the last century at the heart of the departments of Protestant theology. It is, therefore, an event of western culture, and I would even say, of western theology.

That quote is from an anthology of his work edited by Charles Reagan and David Stewart called "The Philosophy of Paul Ricoeur", 1978 and I'm reading from page 215.

And what, according to Ricoeur, is the relationship between theology and a philosophical anthropology based on a re-reading of Marx? The confrontation of theology with

Marxism in particular, he argues, will bring us to discover the question of evil and the question of salvation in a reading of the great forces that regulate our economic life, our political life, and our cultural life. We would not be going very far in an understanding of being lost or being saved, he says, if we could not read this condition in the great stories told by institutions and by structures. So the relationship between Anthropology and Theology, in short, centres on ideological iconoclasm—the shattering of cultural illusions.

What is the practical value, then, of pure research? I think it was John Dewey who said that the essence of all philosophy is the philosophy of education, the study of how to have a world. And that is tied up with the whole question of what it means to be human. And a human being is surely a lot more than a cultural being. But not unless one figures it out. And in order to figure it out, we require some kind of vehicle that transcends culture. Otherwise, we can never get from a cultural perspective to a global perspective. Because to say, for example, that a people is savage or civilized on the basis of something like their eating habits is to express nothing more than a cultural opinion. I mean, what's the difference between taking the people you kill and putting them in the ground and burying them, and taking the people you kill and putting them in the oven and eating them? It's just a matter of taste. Ask any Hindu, especially if he's a high caste Hindu, and he'll probably tell you the idea of eating the flesh of a cow is revolting. But we do that—because we are conditioned to do it. That's why some people eat the flesh of a cow and others don't eat the flesh of a cow, why some people ate the flesh of a human and others didn't eat the flesh of a human: cultural conditioning. A chunk of flesh, be it from one animal species or another, once it's dead, is a chunk of flesh. That dying seaman on Bligh's little boat had that one figured out—and he was no cannibal. The real issue, surely, is not what you do with a body after you kill it, but the fact that you killed it in the first place. And it is ideology that justifies the killing!

After Bligh was exonerated by the British Admiralty and found blameless for losing his ship, he searched out a few of his Bounty mutineers in Tahiti and had them killed—all because they decided there were things they would rather do than risk their lives taking him around the Horn. And he was able to do that because he had the weight of the British Admiralty behind him. Now, from the perspective of pure research, I ask you, is that civilized? Or is it savage? Or am I just being pedagogic and elitist?

AH, SULI!

Talk presented at a United Nations Conference
for Development Agencies, Vancouver, 1984

I want to tell you a story that illustrates some of the human factors associated with the question of reforestation. It's about a tree project that is taking a long time to get off the ground. That's not only because trees take a long time to grow. It's because the human cycle that leads to deforestation takes a long time to reverse. It's a project that is currently underway in the northern part of West Bengal along the border with Nepal. And, as many of you know, this is an area where the mountainsides have been laid bare because the local people are cutting down the trees and using them for firewood.

Now, there's no point telling poor people not to cut down trees. Many of them already know that stripping the mountainside leads to erosion that causes landslides and threatens the villages. These people don't set out to do themselves in. They cut down the trees because they choose life . . . because there's no other source of fuel for preparing their food. Hunger is a much more immediate problem than deforestation.

So this, briefly, is the story of one man's efforts to get a whole lot of people—both in India and in Canada—to do something to reverse the cycle. He is Father Murray Abraham, a Jesuit priest from Cape Breton, Nova Scotia. In 1948, Father Abraham went out to India as a teacher in northern West Bengal. While there, he saw people who, because of geography and economic circumstance, had no access to the formal educational system, nor to the knowledge, skills and resources that would help them get things turned around. So he determined to work for them. He went out into the surrounding villages and gathered together the poorest of the poor, and together, with their bare hands, they removed the rocks from the side of a mountain and turned them into a school. No ordinary school, mind you, but a place where children and adults alike could learn not only literacy and numeracy but also how to produce and market food, and how to raise cows and pigs and chickens. They've now got 40,000 chickens on the roof of the school! And he has financed all of this by convincing 1,200 Canadian families to give up their Friday night dessert and send him the money.

Well that addressed the food problem and made them a lot more self-reliant. But they were still left with the problem of deforestation. So Father Abraham tried to think of ways to keep them from cutting down the trees. There was one old gentleman, for example, who used to cut down three trees every day. That's how he made his living—by selling firewood. So Father Abraham found out how much he earned from this and then hired him as a night watchman for the same amount. He didn't need a night watchman. But three trees a day—that's ninety trees a month, and over a thousand trees a year. From just one man! But how many night watchmen can you hire! And somebody else probably went out and cut down those same trees anyway. So what do you do! I mean, what have you got that you can use. Because the only thing Father Abraham had plenty of was—chickens!

A chicken is not a very smart animal. But it's a useful little creature because it produces eggs. You can sell those eggs to the hotels in Darjeeling—that's where the tourists come to see the Himalayas—and with the money you can buy wheat and rice and dahl (lentils). And that's what they did, because, in Canadian equivalent, one egg is worth $2.80 and that's a lot of money. But those chickens were producing something a lot more valuable than eggs: chicken waste. And with 40,000 chickens they had buckets and buckets of it. In the Nepali language they call it suli. That's a pretty word and certainly a lot nicer than the word we usually call it in English. If you lose an argument, you can say, "Ah, suli!" without also losing your dignity!

But what do you do with all that suli? Well, they used some of it for fertilizing their vegetable gardens. But they had way too much left over and they had to get rid of it, so they started dumping it into the river. And downstream are all those famous Darjeeling tea plantations! One day Father Abraham was apologizing to one of the plantation owners for pouring chicken waste into the water supply, and the guy said, "Hell, no, we irrigate with that water and since you've been doing that, our tea has grown better than it ever did before." Think about that the next time you have a nice cup of Darjeeling tea!

Well, necessity is the mother of invention, and that got Father Abraham thinking. He soon realized that the solution to his deforestation problem was the very stuff he had been throwing away. So he started building "fermenters" to convert the chicken waste into methane gas. And it's really working. When they can produce enough of that stuff, and get it into circulation, then the people won't have to cut down the trees anymore. And that's the time you can start replanting the mountainside.

Now, this may all seem a bit depressing because it's such a long cycle. You can't replant the mountainside until the people no longer need to cut down the trees. And they need to cut down the trees until they get the methane gas. And they can't get the methane gas until they've produced the chicken waste. And they can't produce the chicken waste until they've raised the chickens. And they can't raise the chickens until they've been given the skills and resources to do it. So you need somebody who can put all of this together. And it has to be somebody who realizes, at the same time, that the people themselves are the ultimate resource. That's the encouraging thing about it: the people who are the source of the problem turn out to be the means to its solution. This is development in human terms. It may take a bit longer to get it all going. But once it's in place, chances are it's going to last for a very long time.

POSITIVE PREJUDICE

Talk presented to Volunteers of
Canadian Crossroads International
Vancouver, 1985

I have a real passion for this cross-cultural stuff and I get to talk to a lot of people who are embarking on the kind of adventure you are undertaking here. I always like these occasions and yet, there is something about this particular one that strikes a really somber note in me. It has to do with the particular program you are going on and the person who has just introduced me. You see, twenty years ago I was in the same situation your Director is in now. I was chosen by my University to go on this program. Back then it was called "Operation Crossroads Africa". I was really excited about it; I wanted to do it more than anything else in the world—but my parents said no. Now, I thought I was really clear about this Crossroads thing, and I thought I knew why I wanted to do it. But I was 19 years old—still a minor in the strict sense of the word—so I chose to respect my parents' wishes. I gave up the assignment because they couldn't live with the idea of my being over there with those black people.

That summer, at home in Canada, I did a lot of reflecting about why I was so keen to go and they so keen that I not go. I mean, we all grew up in the same family; we shared the same experiences. Yet they were prejudiced—and I wasn't!

Or so I thought. Because now, with twenty years of hindsight and the vantage point of Anthropology, I realize the reason I was on "go" was because of prejudice. Positive prejudice—but prejudice nevertheless. It's easy to see the negative kind; the other one is more subtle. But they're two sides of the same coin. To illustrate this, I'm going to tell you some stories about my past—positive and negative. You'll get the connection, and then you can apply the principle to your own circumstances.

Now prejudice has deep cultural dimensions and we have to start by situating things there. My parents were born early in this century and grew up in the twenties and thirties. I was born in the forties and grew up in the fifties and sixties. There were some very critical things, culturally speaking, taking shape during those decades. And you are a product of those cultural processes.

For my family, as for most Canadians at that time, a pretty powerful influence was what was going on south of the border. It was particularly critical in my case because during my formative years, the life and work of my family—(we were professional performers)—took us to the United States, and I spent a good part of my early years there. In those days, black people sat at the back of the bus and in the balcony of the church.

It struck me as odd—but everybody seemed to go along with it.

On one occasion, when I was six years old, we were traveling by car through Alabama and we stopped at a gas station. I had to go to the bathroom so my mother told my older sister to take me. As we made our way I noticed there were two ladies restrooms. One said, "White", the other "Colored". My sister headed us toward the one labeled "White". I said, "Let's go to the coloured one." "Why would you want to go to the coloured one?" she said. I replied, "Why go to a plain white washroom when you can go to one that's in colour?" She stopped short in her tracks, stared at me and in a very admonishing tone, exclaimed, "Don't be so stupid! That washroom is not in colour. It's for coloured people!"

I didn't even think of that! I was so naïve. Thank God! My sister had it right—but I think she was wrong. I didn't tell her at the time. She was a lot bigger than me.

It was such a blatant form of prejudice. Yet if you asked most people there if they were prejudiced, they would probably have said no. The exception might be people like those in the Ku Klux Clan, and we feel repulsed by what they say and do. Maybe we have such a strong reaction because they mirror something we don't want to look at—or cannot see—in ourselves. Something that is repressed . . . .

The thing about repressed material is that it comes out in other ways, like slips of the tongue, forgetfulness, humour. For example, something got repressed in the American psyche after the space shuttle disaster. And guess what! A whole lot of Challenger jokes appeared. You've probably heard them. "Question: Why did the astronauts not take a bath before lift-off? Answer: Because they knew they would wash up on the coast of Florida later in the day." Relieves tension. A lot of them had to do with the civilian on board. It was more traumatic somehow for a schoolteacher to be killed because the others were military people. And the thing about military people is that we pay them to do the dying for us. Heard this one? "What's the big deal about the school teacher? It's not the first time a teacher blew up in front of the class."

In Canada, we have ethnic jokes about the people of Newfoundland. We call them Newfie jokes. "Did you hear the one about the Newfie who died and wanted to be buried at sea? Six men drowned digging his grave." That's funny? We've got it that the people of Newfoundland haven't quite got the smarts. It's interesting to look at the derivation of some of these pre-judgements. For example, in an IQ test back in the 50's, the children in Newfoundland scored consistently lower than children in other parts of Canada. Know why? Because there were a series of questions on the test relating to and based on a knowledge of apples and oranges. In the 50's, there were no oranges imported into Newfoundland.

Similar pre-judgements are attributed to black people in the United States. Here's a joke. Adam and Eve are sitting around in the Garden of Eden and, probably because there is nothing better to do, they muse about whether they are black or white. Not able to ascertain it on their own, Eve suggests Adam go up the mountain and ask God. Which he does. He comes back and he says to Eve, "We are white." Eve says, "Is that what God told you?" and Adam replies, "Well, He didn't just come out and say 'You are white'; He said, 'You are that you are'." And Eve says, "How on earth does that mean we are white?" and Adam replies, "Well, if we were black, He would have said, 'You is that you is'."

My brother told me that one. He used to tell me racial jokes because I had such a reaction to them. But since I've been teaching Anthropology, I've paid more attention to them. So he keeps telling them to me—but now he calls it research.

That "I Am" joke—you will remember that God told Moses His name was "I am that I am"—it refers not to racial inferiority but to racial inequality. That's why we joke about it. It releases some of the tension because we know damn well the America black does not get a fair shake. We put them where they are—and we keep them there. Jokes literally spell it out.

Take this one, for example. It came from the time of school desegregation and forced busing in the United States. A white driver has a busload of black and white kids who are, racially speaking, fighting it out. He's fed up. Stops the bus. Makes them all get out and gives them a hell of a lecture. "From now on," he says, "no more black and no more white. You're all . . . green. Do you get that? Green. Not black, not white, all green! Okay? So now, no more fighting. Get back on the bus. Light green in the front; dark green in the back."

All of this is about prejudice. Easy to see, eh? Because it's pretty negative stuff. We don't subscribe to it so we think we are not prejudiced. But the other form doesn't show up quite so easily. The kind I had. What I call 'positive prejudice'. I remember a couple of early childhood events connected to it. One was something given to me by my Sunday school teacher—a songbook that had a picture of Jesus sitting in a circle with a group of children from around the world. And on the opposite page, the hymn, "Jesus loves the little children. All the children of the world. Red and yellow, black and white, they are precious in his sight. Jesus loves the little children of the world." I never forgot that.

And then there was the Grade V Geography textbook called "Visits to Other Lands". There were stories about children from all over the world. On the final exam, there was this question: "Of all the children, which would you most like to be, and why?" My sister got to Grade V ahead of me and she answered, "Olga, from the fjords of Norway, because of all the countries, that is the one most like mine." When I got the same question two years later, I figured that must be the right answer because my sister had passed the exam. But by this time, I was starting to think for myself, and I answered, "Bunga, from the jungles of Malaya, because of all the countries, that is the one most unlike mine." I passed too. Once again, my sister was right—but I thought she was wrong. I didn't tell her, though, because she was still a lot bigger than me.

I grew up with these ideas in my head, and, as a result, I developed a full-fledged positive prejudice. That's why I was on "go" for Crossroads Africa. I went out of my way to be with people of another race. I preferred them, traveled to live and work with them, defended them, fought their causes . . .. Like my dear parents—and my older sister—I was full of prejudice. It was just part of being human.

Or was it? Are we prejudicial by nature? Is it just a part of what it means to be human? Well, it certainly is a part of the human experience because it's pretty much a universal phenomenon. But we are not prejudicial by nature. We are prejudicial by culture. I grew up in the world of my parents—and my sister. If they inherited a slightly different version of it, well they were older than me, and the times, they were a changin'!

So what does prejudice turn on? And how do we get beyond it? Well, it turns on our cultural conditioning. That's clear enough. But getting beyond it is trickier, because it means getting beyond culture. And before you can get beyond it, you've got to see through it. And that's a matter of right education. Not the kind you get in school, mind you. That's training—and that's a large part of why we are prejudiced in the first place. Schooling teaches us to discriminate, to divide the whole into parts, to put things into categories. In other words, it conditions us to judge. And our cultural institutions perpetuate those judgments. They just carry us along. I mean, it just didn't occur to a lot of people that it was down right unfriendly to have blacks sitting at the back of the bus and in the balcony of the church. They were conditioned to it.

It's still going on. Last night on American television—after the news about the thwarted peace march by blacks in Alabama—were the NAACP image awards. Interesting title: National Association for the Advancement of Colored People. Not even 'Black is beautiful' which at least had a bit of a ring to it. But the problem, you see, is in stressing the differences. Creating positive prejudice. Perpetuating boundaries where none should exist.

The peculiar thing about a boundary is that it actually marks off an inside versus an outside. Think about it. Every major religious tradition has asserted that in ultimate reality there are no boundaries. The problem is that we create a map, complete with boundaries, of the territory of nature—which is an unqualified unity—and then we mistake the map for the territory. So the point is not to separate the opposites—black and white (dark green, light green)—and then try to make positive progress, but rather to unify the opposites by discovering a place, a context, if you will, that transcends and encompasses them both. That ground of being would be unity consciousness.

So the goal is not freedom from the negative, but freedom from the pairs, negative and positive. It is the inherent possibility in every major religious tradition, freed, of course, from its institutionalized constraints and distortions. In Buddhism, it is Nirvana; in Hinduism, it is moksha; in Zen, it is satori; in Christianity, it is discovery of the kingdom of heaven within. It is freedom, it is liberation, it is enlightenment, and it brings home the inescapable conclusion that there is no separate self apart from the world. We have always assumed that we are separate from that which we experience, but the moment we actually go in search of that separate self, it vanishes into the experience itself.

What does it all mean? It means that there is absolutely nothing to pre-judge—because there is no separate self to do the judging. Like all boundaries, a separate self is just an illusion. You can't get rid of an illusion; you can only understand it and see through it. Then you realize it is not really there. So as you head off to those far places where the people seem to be most different from you, you have a unique opportunity to transcend the boundaries, to see past the artificial distinctions of race and colour, and to experience that place, that context, where you are truly one with the world.

Away you go!

ANTHROPOLOGICALLY SPEAKING

Transcript of a Television Interview
about the relevance of Anthropology
Vancouver, 1986

Q: Anthropology. Why is it important?

A: Well, in the scheme of things, it's probably not very important at all. We're a nothing planet in the corner of the universe, and whether we burn ourselves up or get burned up by the sun some ages hence, it probably matters very little. But for the 5 billion people who live here, not to mention other life forms as well as those yet unborn, it matters a great deal. We are the first generation with the capacity to destroy our life support system. We have 30,000 nuclear weapons—far more than even a fool could justify. We have different ideologies and social systems, and we're running up against each other. If we're going to survive as a species and continue to live on this planet, we're going to have to learn to get on together. And in order to do this, we had better understand ourselves— and each other.

Now, Anthropology, as the study of humankind, would appear to be a particularly relevant discipline to this end. It proposes to study human culture in all of its aspects, in the past, present and future. That may make Anthropology the most presumptuous of the social sciences, but be as it may, it provides new insight into the nature of human consciousness.

There are at least two schools of thought regarding the value of this new insight and both are valid. The first refers to the idea that we are the way we are because that's the kind of species we are. We're programmed this way because our brains are this way. Birds have birdbrains and therefore act the way birds act. Puppy-dogs have puppy-dog brains and act the way puppy-dogs act. And humans have human brains and act the way humans act. Not that you can do very much about it, but at least you can understand what's beneath it all, and it helps us to better know ourselves and to be accepting and understanding of each other. We will be able to see that our cultural differences are all variations on the theme of being human. In this sense, Anthropology is broadening. It promotes international and cross-cultural understanding. It gets us out of our ethnocentrism and we can see that different customs, beliefs and traditions are equally valid.

The second school of thought refers to the idea that what we've got in our heads, culturally speaking, is a whole lot of stuff that's been made up. Somebody made it up and we bought into it. Like we've got it that Betty Windsor is a queen so we treat her like a queen. She gets more and better housing, more and better food, more and better status and wealth and privilege. And we go along with it because we haven't seen through it. It's like the emperor's new clothes. Of course, she believes it too so she acts like a queen. She dresses for the part and she doesn't show up at the beach in a bathing suit or go to the movies. So it's the idea that society carries us along, telling us who we are and how we should act. The contribution of Anthropology in this view is liberation. It offers a process of critical reflection whereby one can see through the illusive constructs of culture, thereby freeing oneself to the degree possible from the constraints of the social world. Put another way, the promise of Anthropology is the experience of emancipation by means of critical insight into relationships of power, the strength of which lie, in large part, in the fact that these relationships have not been seen through. Rather than generating theories to justify the organization of society, the goal is to free people from it. In this sense, Anthropology is an emancipatory social science.

Q: How do you see your role as an anthropologist?
A: Well, to begin with, I always remind people when they ask me this question that I'm just working on myself. I want to have my life and have it abundantly. (Somebody else talked about that.) So I don't see myself as having a role per se. I have no mission or message apart from life itself. Having said that, in my professional capacity as an anthropologist, the task is to educate. And that, for the most part, is what anthropologists do. Now unfortunately there's not a lot of education going on. There's a lot of training but very little education. If we examine the root of that verb, to educate, we will see that it means "to lead out". So to educate, in my mind, is to create an environment

where critical thinking can take place. It's not about what to think but about how to think. It lets us step back and look in on our social systems and see them for what they are. This is what I hope students will take away from an Anthropology course they do with me.

Q: What can an average person learn from Anthropology?
A: Well, to begin with, there is no such thing as an average person. Each one of us is a unique and totally unrepeatable event in the history of the cosmos. This is highly significant and entirely inconsequential. However, we are all members of a single species, so maybe we can ask what Anthropology can offer to the species as a whole. And I would say at least two important things.

First, Anthropology helps us to understand other cultures. That's important because we travel to faraway places and people from faraway places travel here. So Anthropology helps us to solve the riddles of culture and make sense of what at first hand may appear bizarre, perhaps even frightening. Anthropology helps us to enjoy our differences rather than fear them. And second, Anthropology helps us to understand ourselves. That's important too. It's very useful to know where we've come from, culturally speaking, and to think very carefully about where we're going. We should take a very critical look at our social institutions and our belief structures, and choose what to take and what to leave in our journey from this point in time. Anthropology provides the skills and categories that allow us to undertake this kind of inquiry.

Q: How did you become an anthropologist?

A: Well, I didn't set out to be an anthropologist. I set out to be a missionary. Looking back on it now, I even know why. I remember when I was a child growing up in Nova Scotia, a missionary on furlough came to speak at our church. He had just spent six years in India. He talked about all the false gods they had, and about their primitive notions of medicine. He told about a local healer who grew the fingernail of the small finger on his right hand extra long so that he could reach down and clean out the throats of those coming to him with respiratory infections. I never forgot that, and then he said the benediction in Hindi and that really blew my mind.

He was encouraging people to go to India and I thought that was my style so when I graduated from high school I went to university and studied Psychology and Religion. Well, in the process of translating the Old Testament in Hebrew, I read between the lines. I discovered that the Old Testament is an anthropological monograph about a group of pastoral nomads in the Middle East. At the same time, I was studying Comparative Religion and was really taken with the wisdom of Buddhism and the Hindu Vedas, so I soon knew I couldn't be a missionary. But I was still concerned about the guy who put his finger down people's throats so thought I had better choose a more practical path. I chose international development, and took a Masters degree in Social Work. During that program of study I traveled to Micronesia and took a look at the development programs being operated in those Pacific Islands by the US Department of the Interior. (Micronesia was and still is, in part, a UN Trust Territory under the jurisdiction of the United States.) And when I saw the impact of those programs, I knew I couldn't do development either. They were acculturating those islands and making people dependent on imported goods. So I came into Anthropology to study the whole area of Christianity and international development, especially between Canada and the Third World. I did my doctoral dissertation on missionization and development in the Fiji Islands. I spent almost two years in Fiji doing that, living in a grass hut on an outer island. But I did get to India too. In fact, I went there three times during my PhD program. Interesting, looking back on it now. First I wanted to go there to convert. Then I wanted to go there to help. And when I finally went there, I went to learn. On my very first visit, I checked into the Ramakrishna Mission Institute of Culture in Calcutta and studied there for four months. It was very broadening; it called into question my whole definition of reality. And that's what I like about Anthropology. It just keeps peeling off the layers of cultural conditioning, and I get rid of a lot of cultural baggage. I like to travel light.

Q: Why are you critical of religious institutions?
A: Because they carry us along, you see. Now let me just point out that I make a clear distinction between being religious and

the institutionalization of religion. To be religious is to be very sensitive to life, so sensitive that what people say would be equal to what they do. This would spell an end to organized religion as we know it, because we would have no need for it and people would not subscribe to it in any case.

But we're not there yet. There have been a few figures in history who have tried to point this out to us—Jesus, the Buddha, Ramakrishna . . . but we don't get it at the level they're saying it. So we turn their messages into beliefs and rituals and end up with organized religion. We're confusing the map for the territory.

This would present no problem if we didn't fight over it. But we've got Catholics versus Protestants and Muslims versus Jews. People will argue—even kill and die—for their belief systems. It's a most amazing phenomenon. Because to hold things at the level of belief is a very low level of certainty. Not worth dying for. I mean, the idea is to have your life, not to lose it. If it's going to cost you your life, better think again.

You see, our customs and traditions become ends in themselves. We can see this is the way we treat people in certain cultural roles. For example, we give ordained people the title "Reverend" and make sure we don't swear in front of them. Remember a while back when the news media made a big deal about how many Mercedes the Rajneeshis bought for their guru? People just couldn't understand how those devotees were taken in like that. But we do the same thing. We brought a guy over here not too long ago. We made special pope-mobiles for him, chartered a jetliner and helicopters, gave him the red carpet treatment . . .. It set us back a few million. Fascinating! There's a lovely line in a Woody Allen movie "Hanna and her Sisters" where a guy says, "If Jesus were to come back today, he would never stop throwing up."

We do this with other cultural figures as well—for example, the way we treat so-called "royals" at public expense when they come here while some Canadians have so little. Native people, some of whose land became so called "crown land" (an interesting designation) even come out and dance for them. Well, it's a very interesting cultural phenomenon.

Q: What will the global society be like?

A: We don't have to wonder what it will be like. We just have to notice what's going on right now. We're in the midst of a new revolution. It's difficult to see because it is a quiet one, but it is quickly changing the way we are having our world. This new revolution is the communication revolution. It's the third major revolution. The first was agricultural; the second was industrial. We are shaping this new revolution with computer chips and telecommunication satellites—and it in turn is shaping us.

Now the interesting thing is that this process is deepening our cultural identities and making us global citizens at the same time. This is because the information is instantly available at both the local and international levels. So while we can be linked up with just about anywhere on the planet—and this makes us a global community—we can, at the same time, use this same technology to reinforce local cultural identities, such as the use of computers in the preservation of native languages in Canada. So what we can see is the formation of what I call a "uniculture" with a lot of cultural diversity within it—as opposed to a "monoculture" where everything would be the same.

The other far-reaching implication is that the age of nations is past. Regionalisms on the one hand and the world community on the other are the two emerging social realities as a result of this new revolution. I think we're in for a bit of a stormy time because we don't let go of age-old traditions easily. The challenge is for us to settle all of these conflicts without recourse to violence.

Q: Do you think the human species will survive?

A: Well, if human consciousness could be said to have a singular purpose, it would perhaps be to tell us that a species either adapts to its environment or it dies. Homo sapiens, the creature that we are, has been on the planet for about 40,000 years—perhaps double or even triple that time. But that's not very long in the scheme of things because the planet is probably about 5,000 million years old. And in that long evolutionary journey there have been pre-hominids and early hominids that, for whatever reason, have died out: Ramapithecines, Australopithecines, homo habilis, homo erectus . . .. It is now the era of homo sapiens and it would be both arrogant and naïve of us to think that we are the pinnacle of the evolutionary process. This is just a stage we are going through.

Sapiens means "knowing" or "wise"'; homo sapiens is wise man. Well, as it turns out, wise man is not so wise; he's armed the planet with 30,000 big ones and made everybody a hostage. There's no place on the planet that is safe, and we've got the lines drawn up on the basis of differing social systems and ideologies.

It seems to me that if we are going to get through this, we've got to realize that we are an integral part of the planet. At present, we tend to see ourselves over and against an external world. But the planet is a living organism, and we are a part of that living thing. Recognizing that, in my mind, is more than sapiens—knowing; it is an at-one-ment, atonement. And this is what atonement is. So I call this adapted creature homo sanctus. Sanctus means "holy" and by holy I do not mean beliefs and dogmas and rituals; I mean an at-one-ment with the planet. Now there wouldn't be anything or anyone to fight against because it's all just a part of the whole. There would be unity and where there is unity there is peace.

MECCA FOR THE MODERN-DAY PILGRIM

Talk given at the Department of Anthropology
University of British Columbia,
after the closing of Expo 86 in Vancouver

I would like to begin by saying that this little talk is just for the time being. And the pun is intended, because the human being is a time being, a creature that lives itself out within the context of history. That makes for a rather unhappy situation, actually, because we are, as Plotinus points out, poised midway between the beasts and the gods. The beasts are mortal but would seem either not to know or at least not to appreciate the fact. The gods are immortal and they would appear both to know it and appreciate it. But the poor human being, no longer a beast and not yet a god, is in the worst possible predicament—mortal and knowing it. And the more we have evolved over the millennia, the more conscious we have become of our fate. I am dying—and you are dying too.

That's the first thing: death. Now here's something else. And these ideas might not seem to be connected to the topic but they are. The second thing is life.

Life is evolution and evolution is transcendence. That is to say, with regard to our own species, the development of the psyche has the same goal as natural evolution, which is, the production of ever-higher unities. In other words, if the human species, in the long process of evolution, developed from amoebas, then they are, in the long process of evolution, developing toward God. That's a very optimistic future. But right now we would appear to be somewhere around the halfway mark, and the trick, it seems to me, is to make it through the transition.

Now I guess, before going any further, I should say what I mean by God. Because this is not an attempt to prove the existence of God. It just says what perennial philosophy has been saying all along, that the existence of God is no more improbable than the existence of matter, energy, nature, cosmos . . .. It's just a matter of what you want to call it: Nature, Energy, Spirit, Consciousness, the Tao, the Atman . . .. In other words, it matters not in this context whether all things are forms of Energy, forms of Nature, or forms of God. The point is that this reality or suchness or ground of all being is One, Whole (that's with a "w") and Undivided.

Having said all that, and just keep it in mind, for those of you who were in Vancouver this spring, summer, fall, and especially those who heard the Expo theme song, you will know that there was "something happening, something happening, something happening here". Something, in fact, powerful enough to attract twenty-two million people to our fair city. Again, the pun is intended.

They came from the continents of Africa and Asia and the Americas. They came by plane and train, on boats, buses and in cars. And then there's that most illustrious mode of transportation—the recreation vehicle. They decorated the parking lots with descriptive names like "Explorer", "Discovery", "Viking", "Dreamliner" . . .. And for those who really "don't leave home without it", there was "Midas" and "The Executive". Some even came on foot—and I met one man who cycled all the way from Thunder Bay, Ontario.

Why did they come? Why did they follow the signs that led to Expo? And not only this Expo. There was a world exposition in Tsukuba in 1985. There will be one in Brisbane in '88 and Seville in '92. And there was New York and Osaka and Chicago and Paris . . . a world exposition, it seems, almost every year. An annual . . . what? An annual . . . pilgrimage. Yes, that's it. The Expo site was the site of a pilgrimage. And all those millions of people making their way to Vancouver were pilgrims; **pilgrimage**: (def): a journey to a sacred place; a long journey or a search. Please keep that in mind too.

"Proclaim unto mankind a pilgrimage," commanded Allah to Abraham. Or so the story goes. And when the instruction was revealed later to the prophet Mohammed, the annual pilgrimage to Mecca began. They come from the continents of Africa and Asia and the Americas. They travel by plane and train, on boats and buses and cars. (Recreation vehicles? Maybe there's a market to be explored.) And then on foot, donning the white cotton cloth and sandals, and entry into the holy city of Mecca, some having invested their life savings to make the sacred journey.

Mecca is hot and crowded; there are masses of pilgrims. Housing is at a premium, except, perhaps, for the lucky few who can afford the oasis of the Mecca Inter-Continental Hotel. But never mind the inconvenience. Before they leave, they will enter through one of the gates into the Sacred Mosque and circle seven times the black-draped shrine of the Kaaba. (I have a hunch about the origin of the circumambulation. I think it's because the lineup was so long it took about seven rounds to wind your way to the centre.) It is the spiritual climax of the religious life, a close encounter with the symbols of one's individual and collective identity. Every Muslim with means should make the hajj at least once in a lifetime.

Pilgrimage is one of the five pillars of Islam. The other four are belief in one God, regular prayer, almsgiving and ritual fasting. Now those are rather noble activities, wouldn't you say? And they strike me as the domain of a pretty docile people. So I find it difficult to reconcile all this with Muslim fundamentalism and Holy Wars, which are just a veiled form of human sacrifice. Come to think of it, Muslims, along with Christians, have probably killed more people in the name of God than any other people in history. I look at all this and I'm thinking, "What's wrong with this picture?".

Now the crowning glory of Mecca is the Holy Mosque. And the crowning glory of Expo 86 turned out to be, quite appropriately, the Spirit Lodge. In fact, so popular was the

Spirit Lodge that huge lineups formed into circles around that colossal GM structure, with masses of people slowly winding their way to the innermost sanctum. And so constant were these circumambulations that each morning when the Expo gates opened, you could see throngs of people running straight for the Spirit Lodge to get to the front of the line. It was like the ritual prayer signaling the beginning of the Muslim hajj: "Here we come, Oh Allah, here we come!"

At the heart of the Holy Mosque at Mecca is a black stone. At the heart of the Spirit Lodge at Expo is a fire. Both have a story and a history. In the latter, an Indian storyteller sits beside the fire, and when we assemble, he begins:

> Welcome, travelers, welcome to the Spirit Lodge, and to the World Exposition in Vancouver. When I first came to this fair, I was excited about the theme of transportation and communication, and my heart was filled with joy. But then I looked around, at all those machines and the structures of steel and glass. And my mood changed and my heart grew cold with fear. All these machines, do they make us more like humans or more like machines? And then I thought back to my childhood, to a story told to me by my grandmother—about a magic canoe. You get in. You make a wish. Then you take one stroke with the paddle, and you are there.

Then he recounts the movement of the tribe within the context of their technology, and he realizes that, although the content is different, then and now, and them and us, the form is the same. "Because life and the freedom to move are as one."

But what, precisely, is that form, that deep structure, if you will, that manifests itself in a myriad of surface structures? (He doesn't actually use those words.)

The storyteller goes on. "Ah, Raven, trickster, is it you? Is it all your idea? Is this just another one of your illusions? Raven, the giver of life. Because you know that life and the freedom to move are as one."

That's the punch line. But it's not the climax. The real illusion is yet to come. Because, at this point, right there before our eyes, the storyteller steps into the magic canoe, takes one stroke of the paddle—and disappears. They actually disappear the Indian! Now that's highly symbolic but not at all unusual because we have been disappearing Indians on this continent for at least a couple of centuries.

And they interviewed Bob Rogers, the guy who did the Spirit Lodge. He did "Rainbow War" for Canadian Pacific too; he's a very bright fellow. And they said to him, "Come on, Bob, tell us, how did you disappear the Indian?" And Bob replied, "That's not the question. The question is how we make the Indian appear in the first place."

And that is the question. How do we make the Indian appear? Remember the opening scene at Expo? When those symbols of the British Crown (that's crown as in land) came up the Creek in a boat, appropriately enough, to step ashore and reclaim the territory in the name of the monarch? Who appeared to meet them? The Indians. Again! I mean, I can understand their showing up the first time because they didn't know we were going to take their land. But they know it now. And there they are, appearing at the shoreline of what was once their own territory. And they dance! I was looking at all this and I was thinking, "What's wrong with his picture?"

Now when I say "wrong", I don't mean wrong in the sense of morally wrong, although I would not think it at all ethnocentric to pronounce on holy wars and racial inequality. What I mean here by "wrong" is as in oxymoron: two things that don't fit together. Like some word pairs, for example, such as one I already mentioned: "holy wars". Those two words don't fit together. "Military intelligence": that's another one. It's an oxymoron. A couple others are "wilderness management" and "salvation army". In each case, two things that don't fit together. Now take the same principle but make it active. You set out to do something, and what you end up doing is not what you intended to do. The goal and the outcome do not fit together. So what you have actually done is a substitute activity. And I would suggest that the reason there is something wrong with the picture is that, like pilgrimages and world expositions everywhere, Expo 86 is a substitute activity.

Now, why would anybody settle for a substitute activity? Why set out to do one thing and end up doing something else? Well, it has to do with those two things I mentioned at the outset: life and death. Two things that take place in time; in other words, within the context of history.

I'm going to think about history not as events but as the movement of human consciousness: human consciousness is story and the movement of human consciousness is history.

This view of history might not suit the scientific mind. But if you look at history scientifically, as a process of evolution, moving from the amoeba to the reptile to the ape to the man, you are in fact talking about the movement of human consciousness. As Carl Sagan put it, biology is more like history than it is like physics.

According to a psychologist named Ken Wilber, the individual being, from the very start, contains all the deep structures of consciousness. This is not to say that the infant is enlightened. What it says instead is that the human being has both the potential and the drive, in short, the propensity for it. We need only to actualize it, and perennial philosophy describes the process variously as Nirvana, samadhi, Zen enlightenment, a state of bliss, etc. But in order to attain enlightenment—and here's the crunch—one would need to die to the separate self, to that culturally constructed ego. Because, as I pointed out earlier, that ground of being—God or whatever you want to call it—is One, Whole and Undivided.

Now according to another psychologist, named Ernest Becker, consciousness of death, not sex, is the primary repression. The self that is doomed to die—and knows it—spends a good part of its life (consciously or unconsciously) trying to deny it.

One of the results of this repression or one of the ways of doing this repressing is to create immortality symbols that promise to transcend death. As Becker puts it, the human erects cultural symbols that do not age or decay to quiet his fear of his ultimate end. So culture becomes the antidote for the terror of death, and it shows up in the form of immortality projects. So while each of us wants that essential unity, we want it under conditions that in fact prevent it. Instead of finding timeless wholeness, we substitute the wish to live forever. Put another way, we might say that nature is what a unified Self does with life, and culture is what a separate self does with death. That is why the serious seeker of enlightenment in any tradition has to move outside the cultural system.

Now, depending on how you look at it, immortality projects can be positive or negative. And they can be mythical as in the pilgrimage to Mecca, or rational as in the pilgrimage to Vancouver. We can worship God, or pray or fast or give alms, or we can search for wealth or fame or power or knowledge, all of which tend to imbue us with a sense of immortality. But they are substitute objects just as the separate self is a substitute subject.

Like the scene at Mecca: the pilgrim seeks union with the One, the Whole, the Undivided but under conditions that prevent it. There, in all his ideological separateness, in a place where only the Muslim can come, he substitutes his sought-for unity with symbols of limited identity.

Like the scene at Expo: the world coming together in Vancouver? No, a world divided—into provincial, national, state and corporate entities. There, in all their separateness, all boxed in, operating within the artificial boundaries they set for themselves. Displays of wealth and power and fame and knowledge. Somewhere inside each of those pavilions was reference to the first, or the best, or the biggest or tallest— something! One I found amusing was Yugoslavia's claim to be the top spot for hospitality to Rick Hansen; it was "hospitality that was second to none". They were proud to be Australians, and they were proud to be Canadians. There was "no place like Saskatchewan", and British Columbia "has it all".

But life and the freedom to move are as one—and the nations are all on the move. Singapore is on the move. Korea is on the move. Everybody is on the move, moving—somewhere. The traditional societies are moving from rural environments into cities, and the industrialized societies are moving from urban environments into space. Norway is moving into the sea.

Nowhere was this whole process more pronounced than in the American and Russian pavilions. I want to take these two as a case in point because there are perhaps no two national groups that go to such pains to say they are different. And they were very competitive about the whole Expo thing, great secrecy on both sides in the planning stages.

They get the prize, incidentally, for being the most alike. That shouldn't surprise us, really, because they think a lot about each other and are very interested in what each other is doing. But the final products could not have been more alike if they were a collaborative effort. For example, both pavilions were designed so that one had to enter on the upper floor, both exhibited the latest in space technology and featured space stations. And both were crowned on the exterior by timeless monuments to technological disasters associated with space exploration: for the one, a sculpture of Yuri Gagarin—half man, half angel (that's interesting!)—who was killed on a hard landing when his parachute didn't open; and for the other, a stylized rendering of the initials "USA" in the form of the ill-fated Challenger space shuttle. Talk about immortality symbols! In fact, so alike were these two, that at the closing ceremony, they broke rank and walked together into BC Stadium, flag in flag, hand in hand. People cheered. Like there was "something happening, something happening, something happening here". And there was—a movement toward the creation of a higher unity—for life and the freedom to move are as One, as Whole, as Undivided.

How to sum this all up? According to perennial philosophy, one's essential nature is not everlasting; rather, it is timeless. So liberation does not mean living forever; it means instead a direct and immediate apprehension of the spaceless and timeless Ground of Being. But it takes a lot of dying to get to that level of living. And dying is not what we do best. In fact, we deny death, and we set up immortality projects in our attempts to prevent it.

Life and the freedom to move are as One, as Whole, as Undivided. Until we awaken to that Unity, we will dream in our separateness. We will go on pilgrimages and fight holy wars, have land disputes and world expositions.

Dreaming: a substitute activity for the time being, that remarkable and absurd little creature who was probably born too soon.

MAY A LITTLE CHILD LEAD YOU

Talk given to Staff of the United Nations Pavilion,
World Expo 88, Brisbane, Australia
prior to Opening on April 30, 1988

You have already learned about what's going to be inside the United Nations Pavilion at World Expo 88. So I'm going to talk to you about three programs that are extensions of the pavilion but that do not take place inside the building as such. They consist of an upper primary and junior secondary schools program, an ongoing series of items on children's television, and an Australia-wide contest for kids. Listen to these titles: Crisis in Space Village, World Games, Worldwatch Reports, How I Would Put the World Right, and My Idea for a Better World. Adventurous and very exciting! But this is heavy subject matter. Why are we involving children in the problems of the world?

Well, this is a world exposition. And pavilions at a world exposition usually address two central questions. First, they tell us who they are. Or who they've got it that they are! Or who they want you to think they are! For example, my hunch is that the Australian Pavilion will talk about Aborigines and glorify their dreamtime, even though these same Aborigines have never been incorporated into Australian society. The Canadian Pavilion will have totem poles, clan symbols of the very people whose land we stole. And Queensland, well, the Pavilion will probably tell you that up here in the sunshine state it is beautiful one day, perfect the next, even if it is pouring rain outside.

That's about question one. The second question that pavilions at a world exposition address is where they are going. Or where they've got it that they're going! Or where they want you to think they're going! Now this one gets a bit trickier because, as the physicist Niels Bohr puts it, "Prediction is very difficult, especially about the future." So the pavilions will feature prototypes of things to come, and years from now, when we look back in retrospect, some of them will strike us as pretty funny.

Well, what about us? Who are we—and where are we going? We are the United Nations Pavilion; we represent the people of the nations. And the people of the nations are one in a million living species on a living planet. The name of this species is homo sapiens. Homo means "man" and sapiens means "wise". So homo sapiens is the so-called wise man and he has been on the planet for more than 40,000 years. He follows in the evolutionary path of homo erectus ("upright man") and homo habilis ("tool-making man"). Homo sapiens is a clever little creature; so clever, in fact, that he has become the dominant species on the planet. And that is no mere achievement.

At the present time, there are just over five billion of us. In fact, the five billionth person was born on July 11th of 1987. Over five billion and world population grows by 150 per minute. So when World Expo 88 opens on April 30th at 10:00 a.m., the world population clock at the United Nations Pavilion will begin ticking at 5,063,378,000. And that figure will increase by 150 per minute. 150 per minute, that's 220,000 per day, 80,000,000 per year. That means, at the present rate of growth, world population will reach 6 billion before the end of this century, 7 billion by the year 2010 and 8 billion by the year 2020. Now, I have some good news and some bad news. The good news is that world population growth is slowing down. The bad news is that it could be over 100 years before it levels off, and by that time, the present world population will have doubled.

Well, that's who we are. Now, where are we going? That's a tough one to call. But given the direction in which we are currently headed, chances are we are going to a not good place. Why? Because our ability to use technology outstrips our ability to get along with each other, and as a result, the world is becoming increasingly more dangerous. For example, you've heard about the Chernobyl nuclear disaster. The explosive energy of that accident was 0.1 kilotons. Just keep that number in mind: 0.1. And you know about the bomb we dropped on Hiroshima. The explosive energy of that bit of firepower was 15 kilotons. 15 kilotons: it killed 75,000 people. Now, do you know the explosive energy of the current nuclear stockpile on the planet? Brace yourselves: it's 16 million kilotons. 16 million kilotons: that's enough firepower to kill 15 billion people. It doesn't require an in-depth understanding of mathematics to figure out that's enough to kill every human being on the planet three times. The military jargon for this blatant insensibility is "overkill", and it defies even the wildest application of economic theory about surplus and elasticity of demand. It's a very bad scene—and the kids are watching.

Recently there have been a number of surveys done with American and Soviet children to find out their take on the global situation. The majority of these children do not think that they will live to be adults; they are concerned they will be killed in a nuclear confrontation. Now that's not a lot of incentive for goal setting, is it! In one interview, a little boy was asked what he thought of nuclear weapons. And he said, "They're bad. They're really bad. They are so bad you wouldn't even want to have one in your house." Well, this planet is our house—and we've got 30,000 of them in it. Children do not deserve to be brought up in a house like that. We are unfit parents.

Let's just take a look at how we've put our house in order. In 1986, which was, ironically, the International Year of Peace, global military expenditures reached $900 billion per year. We spend $900 billion every year on the technology of war. When World Expo 88 opens at 10:00 a.m. on April 30th, a monitor at the United Nations Pavilion will indicate that since January 1st of this year, we will have spent $346,800,000,000 on world military expenditures. And that total will increase by $2 million per minute. It's costing us $2 million every minute! At the present rate of world arms spending, the average person can expect to give up four years' salary to pay for it. All this while one adult in three cannot read or write, and one billion live in inadequate housing. Now I have some good news and some bad news again. The good news is that just last year, in 1987, the total grains in stock around the world was 453 million tonnes. That's enough to feed the world's hungry for two years. And now the bad news. While there has never been so much food surplus on the planet, the total number of hungry people is still rising. At least 730 million people do not eat sufficient calories for an active working day, and one in six people on the planet is undernourished.

So who are we? We are homo sapiens, "wise man" who, it turns out, is not very wise. Or, in the more generic and less sexist terminology, we are humankind who, it turns out, is not very kind. And where are we going? Well, if we keep on our present course, we are, as I said earlier, going to a not good place. But we can change course. That is one of the remarkable features of this clever little creature that we are: we can choose. And what do we need to make life-giving choices? We need to reclaim our birthright as "wise" and "kind". And that requires an awakening of our intelligence, a blending of head and heart that allows us to see ourselves as an integral part of the planet and its myriad of life forms.

That's the message inside the United Nations Pavilion. And that's what these extension programs for children are about. We are saying to children—of all ages—that there is something important to discover here. And we are going to let you discover it in a subtle and entertaining way. So now let's find out what's behind those titles.

World Games: a book of simulation games on global issues that teachers can use in the classroom. There's "The Earthling Game"—discovering that all children have the same needs. "The Neighbour Game"—experiencing the world as a global village. "The Culture Game"—seeing ourselves as others see us. "The Refugee Game"—knowing what it's like to be without a country. And "The World Game"—learning that cooperation is essential for survival. All of this is very serious matter—and it's also a lot of fun.

Crisis in Space Village: with Captain Starship and Space Maiden. Don't look at me, I didn't make up these characters; I inherited them. Captain Starship is a faceless fellow; he wears a space helmet to protect from dangerous radiation. I'm curious as to why Space Maiden was not seen to require similar protection. Interesting! Anyway, I asked the people who invented Captain Starship if we could give him a face. "No," they said, "he never has a face. It creates a mystique about him and the kids like it." Some mystique. Just think about it. Who are the faceless people we come to know about? Bank robbers, terrorists and hijackers . . . hardly good role models for children! But you win some and you lose some. Space Maiden wears blue makeup that makes her look as though she has been involved in a domestic dispute. I asked them to clean her up a bit, and they did. And then I sent this space age dual on a mission—to solve the crisis in Space Village. And they, in turn, get the kids—the readers of the Galactic Gazette—to help them. Space Village turns out to be planet earth, of course, and the kids get into the act of figuring out what's the best way to have a world. It's accomplished by providing them with a lot of "Worldwatch Data", factual information about the planet and its inhabitants, so that kids can make informed choices. And the data come by way of a very intelligent computer called C-2020. "C" stands for "computer" and 2020 is the galactic year in which it was made. But, more symbolically, C-2020 means "see with perfect vision". It's all about vision, something we lack because of the interpretations we impose on what we see. C-2020, with his so-called artificial intelligence, can cut through all the distortions and see things for what they are.

Kids Make a Difference. Just like the rest of us, kids feel powerless to do anything that will make a difference. The problems seem too overwhelming both in scope and complexity. So we feature kids who, in their own personal ways, undertake something that represents a personal attempt to shift the balance. For example, here in Australia there is a 13-year-old who has set up a crisis hotline in his home to help kids with their personal problems. And there's the 12-year-old from Melbourne who has established a national coalition against war toys. Another example comes from the USSR: a 12-year-old girl who has been composing poetry since the age of four. "What frightens me is indifference," she said in a recent interview. "It can devour the world, our tiny little planet, the little heart that beats in the universe." Or as she writes in a poem called "Telling Fortunes":

what a shame
that I'm not a fortune teller.
I would tell fortunes
only with flowers
and I would heal the earth's wounds
with a rainbow

Worldwatch Reports. These are factual little gems about places and people that serve to break down our rather ingrained stereotypes. The idea is to create an appreciation for all living things on the earth and to enjoy differences rather than fear them. For example, do you know what is the oldest continuous living culture on the planet? Most people say it is that of the Egyptians or Greeks or Chinese. But the oldest continuous living culture on the planet is that of the Australian Aborigines—a remarkable thing to appreciate about them.

My Idea for a Better World: a contest that gives children across Australia a chance to say how they would like to set things up. And that's no idle task because so much of our action is grounded in ideas. The contest takes its inspiration from a similar one conducted in Canada called "How I Would Put the World Right". There was a wealth of suggestions. Here's one from a 9-year-old: "What I would do to change the world: I would dig up all the bombs and disconnect them." And one from a little boy age 11: "I'd lower the prices of important food like milk, bread and meats, and I would make liver unedible (sic)." And this from an eight-year-old: "I'd send up a plane that carried a sign that said 'Stop All Terrible Things.' That's what I'd do." Here's one: "There should be Cabbage Patch kids for

$30, not $50." And this is rather sobering: "I would stop my mum and dad shouting at each other all the time." That's from a six-year-old.

And here's a final one, a lovely little poem by a ten-year-old girl:

> How I would put the world right
> Is take away all the fright
> Of wars
> And the world's unfair chores
>
> How I would put the world right
> Is give everyone a silent night
> Absolutely no crying
> From babies who are dying

These are the programs that you will want to know about as hosts of the United Nations Pavilion because people may make reference to them or ask you about them. And one more thing: when you are out there on the floor, at the main entrance to the pavilion or in one of the theatres, giving the same little talk time after time and answering the same questions day after day, please remember that the people into whose eyes you look may be hearing the message for the first time. And even when the immensity of that realization fails to sustain you and you look for something to help you carry on, may a little child lead you.

A FOUR-LETTER WORD

Talk to Faculty & Students,
Kelly Commercial College
Brisbane, Australia. 1988

The last time we met, it was the day before Good Friday. You were sitting here as you are now, waiting for your graduation ceremony to end so you could break for the holiday. It was pouring rain and I was lecturing to you about death and destruction. Not a very fitting way to start an Easter break! Or was it? In fact, maybe it was very fitting. Because if you think about it, the purpose of Good Friday is to remember a guy who got himself killed for calling God a four-letter word.

What was the word? (No response) Does anyone know what the word is? (No response) What is the four-letter word that he said God is? God is—what? (A faculty member whispers "love".)

Yes, he said God is love. And I'm not surprised that it didn't jump from your lips because the word is taboo. Have you noticed that people rarely talk about love? They talk about war and hate and violence but they hardly ever talk about love.

And if you go around talking about love, people will start to get suspicious of you.

I spent twelve years schooling. And in all those years I never heard the word "love" mentioned even once. It seemed a rather important thing not to have learned anything about so I thought I would try again and I spent another twelve years in university. I studied disciplines that should have something to say about love: Psychology, Philosophy, Anthropology . . . and I learned a little bit about love from each of them. In Psychology, I found out that babies in an orphanage, when given basic care but no love, died from a disease called marasmus. Four years of Psychology and that's what they told me about love. In Philosophy I found out that the Greeks have a lot of words for love while we have only one. There's agape, godly love, philios, brotherly love and eros, sexual love . . . .. That's what I got from Philosophy. And then in Anthropology I learned that when you introduce money into a traditional society, it makes possible love as a value in itself. Up to that point it doesn't come up—and doesn't need to—because people are tied to each other through a network of kinship obligations. So, as you can see, there hasn't been a lot of research done about love. Yet it would seem to be a rather critical thing because if you don't get any of it, you can die. And there are all kinds of it. And where there is love, there is money. Just keep that in mind.

Now the other thing I talked about last time we met was the United Nations Pavilion at World Expo 88. The Pavilion is all about love. But, of course, we never use the word because, remember, it is taboo. Now the show is up and running and you can go see it for yourself, so I'm going to tell you about something else.

Last week was International Children's Week at Expo so we decided to let the children run the show. We dressed them up in our hosting uniforms and we let them greet the guests, speak in the theatres and press the buttons to start the computers. Who says kids can't run the show! Mind you, they were only 12 years old and they looked kind of little. When they stretched out their arms to point to the exits, the sleeves of their Ken Done sweatshirts almost covered their fingertips. The audience laughed—but they got the message.

Well, the other thing we had these Youth Ambassadors do was conduct a survey to find out what kids their own age think about the world and about their own future. It was interesting because the boys interviewed boys and the girls interviewed girls. If they had been a few years older, it would probably have been the other way around! Anyway, what they found out was consistent with surveys done with kids in other parts of the world. The big thing on kids' minds these days is war—especially nuclear war. They're also concerned about pollution of the environment. In short, their big concern about the future is that there isn't going to be one. That's not a lot of incentive for busting your brains in school, is it!

There were some other concerns expressed as well. Some kids are worried that there won't be a job for them when they grow up. Do you know the feeling? They're afraid of growing up and living in poverty. Imagine, in an abundant land like Australia, afraid that you will grow up and live in poverty. And there was a lesser number whose big concern was loneliness. They are afraid that when they grow up they will be lonely. Fascinating! Loneliness on a planet with 5 billion unique—and mostly interesting—people. And even the dull have their story.

Then there were a few wild cards. Like the ten-year-old girl whose biggest concern about the future is that she won't get into law school! And a twelve-year-old boy whose biggest concern about the future is—get this—marriage! Afraid that he will, not that he won't! Actually, he was not a Weetabix kid; he was from New York, and his fear is probably well placed because divorce lawyers are pretty pricy in that town.

Well, those were the unusual ones. But the majority of kids—and they interviewed more than 600 of them—were concerned about war and pollution. And to get things changed around, they want us to do two things: stop fighting and stop polluting. That sounds simple enough. But it presents us with a formidable challenge. Because even if we could get our act together to quit fighting and dismantle all 30,000 nuclear warheads we have stockpiled—we've still got the problem of where we're going to put them.

Well, that's where we are right now. Kids know that. And we don't seem to have the solution. Kids know that too. Surely goodness we're not going to leave it to them to figure out. Maybe it's high time we started using that four-letter word.

A VERY SPECIAL DAY

Talk to Staff of United Nations Pavilion, World Expo 88
Brisbane, Australia. 1988

This talk is dedicated to Vladimir Lyakhov and Abdul Ahad Momand, the two cosmonauts aboard the Soyuz TM-5 re-entry capsule whose drama in space yesterday reminds all of us to protect and appreciate life.

It is Thursday, September 8th, 1988. I think it is very fitting that we should begin this special day together. I don't know if you appreciate how special this day is. But there are at least a couple of human beings on this planet who appreciate today probably more than any day they have lived before.

Two cosmonauts, one from the Soviet Union, the other from Afghanistan, happy to awaken to a new day with a full 24-hour supply of oxygen, not to mention food, water and toilet facilities. Things got to a critical point yesterday when the guidance system on their re-entry module malfunctioned. They were fast running out of air and there was no food. At best, they had only a couple of days to live.

Against the odds—because two out of three attempts at

re-entry failed—they made it safely to another spaceship. Not back to the Mir space station where the other cosmonauts were hanging out, but to a much larger one still, with five billion space travelers on board. Some spaceship, eh! But incredible as it sounds, there's enough oxygen for all of them, not to mention food, water and toilet facilities—and enough to last even more than a couple of days.

The tiny spacecraft ran amuck because of problems with the guidance system, and the lives of the passengers hung in the balance. We waited and watched, helpless to do anything about it. Then we shared their relief when we found out they came home. Safely home . . ..

Or are they? It may well be that those two cosmonauts have jumped from the frying pan right into the fire. Because the spaceship they're on now also has a fragile guidance system. In fact, we're lucky it has managed to keep us on course up to now.

You see, a spaceship is only as good as its guidance system. And a guidance system is only as good as the minds that build and maintain it. That's why the United Nations Pavilion is here. And that's why you and I are here. We're here to "mind" and "remind" people—including ourselves—that we're riding on a spaceship.

Spaceship Earth: "one ball of rock we call home. It's all we've got—and it's all we need." Do the lines sound familiar? Tired of hearing them by now? Yesterday makes them worth listening to again. It's a reminder that if we want to continue the human journey, we had better build and maintain a solid guidance system. That would mean safeguarding our life supports and passing the food and water around. It would mean getting along with the other passengers and quit making like some of them don't belong here. Above all, it would mean getting rid of the "big ones" and not burning up the oxygen.

There was something very symbolic about what happened yesterday. Think of it: the Soviet Union and Afghanistan—two countries that have been fighting it out lately. But I'll bet you, when that tiny spacecraft ran into trouble there was no political distance between Vladimir and Abdul. Just travelers in space who all of a sudden found themselves on a very tight schedule, facing up to the odds of their living—and dying—together. They showed us what it's like to get to the critical point.

Well, we are also travelers in space, and we are just beginning to realize that we too are on a very tight schedule. We've got to face up to the odds of our living—and dying—together. So it seems to me that unless we build and maintain a solid guidance system, we too will find out what it means to be at the critical point.

"But we do have choices." We can shift ourselves from the critical point to the turning point. **The Turning Point**: the title of Fritjof Capra's book about crisis and transformation, the author taking his inspiration from the book of *I Ching*:

> After a time of decay comes the turning point. The powerful light that has been banished returns. There is movement, but it is not brought about by force . . .. The movement is natural, arising spontaneously. For this reason the transformation of the old becomes easy. The old is discarded and the new is introduced. Both measures accord with the time; therefore no harm results.

Our task, like that of all travelers in space, is to shift from the critical point to the turning point . . . so that the powerful light that has been banished returns . . . so that there is movement that is not brought about by force . . . so that the transformation of the old becomes easy . . . so that no harm results. And so that, along with Vladimir and Abdul, we can— all five billion of us—have a very special day.

PADDLE YOUR OWN CANOE

Talks given to
Agency Chiefs Child and Family Services,
Saskatchewan. 1999

Opening Session

I want to begin by thanking you for inviting me to come here. I am really grateful for this opportunity and in a few minutes, I think you will understand why.

Let me tell you what we are going to do in this workshop. I have put together an outline of some things you might want to consider in making a master plan for taking care of your children. There is a fair bit of material here, perhaps more than we can get through in a couple of days. I will give a copy to your Director. (He's a good man; don't let him get away!) Then you can use the material however you think it might be helpful to you.

I want to begin with a story. It might seem at first to have nothing to do with the topic—but it does. I have here a picture of my father. He is seated in a canoe with his paddle in hand. Beside the picture is a write-up that talks about his life as an athlete and champion canoeist. Over the years, he won many canoe races and received a lot of medals and trophies. He is no longer with us. This is from a Sports Hall of Fame in Nova Scotia, which is where my father was born and grew up.

Everything in the write-up is true. But there is one thing missing: it doesn't say how my father came to be such a great canoe paddler. And the reason it doesn't is probably because the people who wrote it didn't know. But I know — because my father told me. He said he was a champion because he was taught how to paddle a canoe by the Micmac. You see, Europeans — back then, anyway — paddled the canoe with shallow arm strokes. More than that, they would make a few shallow strokes with their arms on one side of the canoe, and the canoe would veer off in the wrong direction. To get it back on course, they would shift to the other side and paddle there for a while. Back and forth . . . and sometimes it was quite amusing to watch them.

But the Micmac, they paddled with the whole body. They sat tall and straight, and made strong deep strokes with their paddles. And with each stroke, before they lifted the paddle from the water, they would steer to keep the canoe on course. They went straight for the goal. These Micmac knew where they were going and how to get there. They had strength and balance and rhythm, and they knew how to work in unison. They knew how to paddle their own canoe.

I never actually met any of these Micmac. In fact, I never met any native people when I was a child. But because of my father, I had a very firm idea what Native people were like. In my mind they stood tall and straight, were very wise and very strong. They knew where they were going and they knew how to get there. They paddled their own canoes.

When I am grown up and it is time for me to go out into

the world, my first real job is as a Case Aide in the Penticton Welfare Office. It is just for the summer as I am on my way to the School of Social Work at the University of British Columbia. It turns out that the Penticton Indian Reserve is on my caseload. (Now, this is very interesting, isn't it: a European man by the name of Christopher Columbus made a geographical mistake 500 years ago and they're still calling you people "Indians".)

The supervisor in the Welfare office says maybe I shouldn't be assigned to the Reserve because it is a pretty tough place for a beginner. I have only a BA in Psychology and I don't know very much about social work. But I say, "Hey, no, I really want to work on the Reserve." Because, you see, I am dying to get out there and meet these wise and strong people who had turned my father into a champion.

On my very first day, I get into one of those big ugly government cars and head straight for the Reserve. I'm so excited; I can't wait to meet them, and they'll be so glad to see me when they hear about the Micmac and all that. I arrive, and . . . guess what: there's nobody there. I mean, the whole Reserve is empty. And then I stop and think, "Well, silly me, of course, it's the middle of the afternoon on a week day. They must all be at their jobs in the city. I'd better come back after the offices are closed."

Well, the very next day I figure out why I didn't see anybody on the Reserve when I drove up in that big ugly government car. They were hiding! Know how I figure it out? Because today my supervisor tells me to go out to the Reserve to serve notice on a family that the Welfare is going to court to keep their children in a foster home in town. I say, "Oh, you can't keep their children in town; they'll miss their families and their village!" to which she replies, "All the Indian children should be in foster homes in town. The Reserve is no place for children."

Is this what social workers do on the Reserve? I'm not going to do that! I drive out to the Reserve, to the home of the Band counselor, a nice lady, and I ask her, "Is there any place on the Reserve where I can bring a child if they are having a problem at home?" And she says, "Well, you can bring them here." And right there on the spot we set up a safe house.

Now an interesting thing starts to happen. When I drive out to the Reserve, people stop hiding. And the children come running to the car. Sometimes they hop inside the car, pull on the seat belts and ask me to take them for a ride. So we go riding. The hills are pretty around there.

After a few days the children from the Reserve start showing up at my office in town. At first they come at the end of the workday and we go swimming. You see, Penticton is situated between two beautiful lakes, but the Reserve isn't near either of them. It's on barren land stuck in the back, past the sawmill. So we have fun swimming together.

Pretty soon the children start coming any time of day, and my office is big enough so I set up a little drop-in centre at one end of it. There are interviewing rooms in the building so they don't interfere in my work. I figure the Welfare office — which is in the courthouse — is probably on stolen Native land anyway so they have a right to be there. I get some paper and crayons and they start drawing pictures and things. It is really a lovely time I have with them. Of course, the administrators in the Welfare office aren't too happy about it. And they don't know how to deal with it because, up to that point, I don't think a Native person had ever stepped inside those doors.

One day one of the teen-age boys walks in, carrying his helmet. (He is driving a motorcycle without a license.) I can hear the receptionist ask him, "Where are you going?" He says, "I'm going to Pamela's office." She says, "You can't go in there. You don't have an appointment." I am listening to all this and I'm thinking, "Appointment! When those Europeans sailed over here in their ships, came ashore and planted their flags in Native soil, did they have an appointment!" Well, I think the people in that Welfare office are glad when summer ends and I leave for the School of Social Work at UBC.

It's a year later now. I've graduated from the School of Social Work and I'm a professional social worker. My first full time position is with the Department of Social Welfare and Rehabilitation in, guess where—right here in Saskatchewan. Heading east on the train, I figure I can handle just about any family situation that I encounter except, perhaps, childbirth. I have to tell you that nothing scares me like the idea of childbirth. I could never comprehend how something with a head that big could come out of an opening that small.

I take up my post in the Child Welfare and Protection Branch of the Regina office. Most of my caseload is Native. I'm a 21-year-old single girl and all of a sudden I have 74 children! Over the next few weeks and months, I see every imaginable problem—but here's the one that takes the cake. One day about 3 o'clock in the afternoon, I get a telephone call from a young Native boy about 10 years old who very calmly and politely asks, "Could you please come out right away. My Mom is having a baby."

I jump into one of those big ugly government cars and head straight for their home, trembling all the way. What am I going to do when I get there! I arrive, hurry inside, and there she is: the mother, up and dressed, holding her new infant which she has washed and wrapped in a clean cloth—and she is feeding the baby sterilized water.

Talk about paddling your own canoe! I cannot tell you how humble I feel at this moment. I think, "Why on earth is the Government of this province paying someone like me to come here to help these people when they are far more capable than I am! Why don't they take that money and put it directly into their hands?" Now you have probably wondered the same thing yourself!

But that's only half of it. Here's the other half: how did these Native people get themselves to the point where they need to turn to this kind of outside help? Have they forgotten who they are? So you can imagine how happy I am to find out that you people have established your own agency . . . to provide your own Children and Family Services. I applaud you—and I want to offer what support I can. That is why I have put together the ideas I want to present to you. They are a humble contribution toward what I hope will some day be a Master Plan for nurturing Cree children in their Native home communities. The purpose is to remind you to paddle your own canoe.

Closing Session

From the material your Director sent to me to help me prepare for this workshop, I learn that the First Nations people of this area want, and I quote:

> "to regain what has been lost over the years"
> "to regain our language, values and traditions"
> "to keep our children in their native home communities"
> "to give our children a brighter future, a sense of belonging and their native identity"
> "(to teach children) the terms of the treaties and to show them how to maintain their treaty rights"
> "to help our children in our own communities"
> "to regain and instill our native culture to our children by our own professionals, parents and elders"
> "to provide the Circle of Life"

In short, they want to move from domination to liberation.

There is a very powerful quotation by the Chinese thinker Lao Tsu that your Director very appropriately has applied to this work. It goes like this: "Just as spring follows winter in nature, so does liberation follow domination in culture."

It is true that everything has its season. Spring does follow winter. This knowledge can serve as hope and inspiration that liberation will follow domination. But there is, I think, a deeper message in this statement. Springtime is a window of opportunity. Because if you plant seeds during the time when the earth is warm and sprinkled with rain, there will be growth. The seeds will blossom and grow into life-giving food. But if the seeds are not planted during this period, it doesn't matter how warm the sun or how gentle the rain; nothing will grow.

As in agri- culture, so in human culture. To shift from domination to liberation means being vigilant so that when the season is right—when the window of opportunity arrives—you are ready to plant. The universe will favour you if you act at the right time. And liberation will be the fruit of your labour.

And what are the seeds you must plant? The knowledge of who you are. Because as you think, so shall you become. It will be easy to dominate you if you forget who you are; it will be impossible to dominate you if you remember.

BOOKED FOR LUNCH

Talk given at Vancouver Public Library,
following publication of
THE CANNIBAL'S COOKBOOK, 1996

Thank you for that kind introduction and for inviting me to speak at this magnificent new library. And thank you, brave souls, for showing up at an event called "Booked for Lunch" when the cuisine is cannibalism and the recipes are for human sacrifice! You might have noticed that the calendar date is auspicious too: we're mid-way between Hallowe'en and Remembrance Day! Scary . . ..

Well relax; we are not going to ask for volunteers. We're not even going to do a cooking demonstration. No, we're going to marvel at how people turn the joy of living into a struggle for survival, and in the process, what they do to each other, not to mention what they do to themselves. It's about human beings, consuming and being consumed by their fellow human beings. Cannibalism. Yes, we are using it as a metaphor.

Now, you'd think that would go without saying, wouldn't you. Well, no. There are some people out there who think this is a how-to book about cooking and eating people. Case in point. I have here an order form from a bookstore in Weyburn, Saskatchewan. Copies of the book arrived at their retail outlet. And what did they do? Promptly sent them back. Not only that, they scribbled a little message on the order form. It reads, and I quote: "We will quit our jobs before we put this book on the shelf." The distributor phoned them and explained what the book is about. "Oh," they said, "I guess we should have looked inside the cover."

One of our business associates was reading the book on his bus commute to work one morning. After awhile, he noticed some people staring at him. Then he overheard them talking. "Did you see the name of that book he's reading?" said one. "Yeah," replied the other, "some people are really sick, aren't they!"

More than they really know, I suspect. Let me give you a few quick figures. Since World War II, which was the war to end all wars, 50 million people have been killed in wars. That's sick! As we speak, 250,000 children are being used as soldiers, many of them to clear land mines because they are expendable. Really sick! Global military expenditures have now exceeded one trillion dollars a year. That's more than $2 million dollars every minute spent on the preparation and execution of war. All this while 1 in 3 adults on the planet cannot read or write, 1 billion people live in inadequate housing and 1 in 5 human beings does not eat sufficient calories for an active working day.

Yeah, some people are really sick, aren't they!

These are blatant examples but as I traveled the world, I saw all manner of human behaviour that was sacrificial. The kinds of things that if you asked people if they would really choose to do that—never mind having it done to them—they would undoubtedly say no. Yet they did it without question. It fascinated me, this cultural conditioning process.

Then something else occurred to me. I started seeing parallels between these strange and exotic customs and things we were doing right here at home. I couldn't see it when I was here. I had to get outside and look in from there. Like the way fish don't see water and birds don't see air, people don't see culture—not their own, anyway. As a result, we follow the dictates of our social systems much as we respond to post-hypnotic suggestion. We're like robots, ready and willing to do and to be all manner of human sacrifice.

I started documenting these stories and making notes on the parallels as I studied my Anthropology. Then as fate—or destiny—would have it, I found myself doing fieldwork in the Fiji Islands. It was supposed to be India. The fieldwork involved researching the pre-contact culture of Fiji, that is, the culture in place before and at the time of the arrival of the missionaries—about 150 years ago.

Fiji at that time was rife with cannibalism, not to mention widow strangling, female infanticide, and other forms of human sacrifice. For example, when they set out to build a new temple, they would sacrifice and bury a human being beneath each of the four corner posts. When a chief wanted to launch a new canoe—these were big sea-going crafts—they would kill a number of men to use as rollers, the victims afterwards eaten as "food for the carpenters".

There are lots of these historical tidbits in the book, by the way. Most of them from a young Wesleyan Methodist missionary named Thomas Williams who wrote one of the best accounts of early Fijian culture. He was only twenty-five years old when he left England for Fiji in 1840. Get this: he got married, ordained and boarded a mission ship for the Fiji Islands all within a few short weeks of each other. It took the ship 299 days to sail from England to Fiji, and you can bet by the time they got there, the honeymoon was over!

I learned a lot from the Rev. Thomas Williams. He was my eyes in early Fiji. He saw what I was not there to see. And he saw plenty of cannibalism. It was all around him. He could look out the window of his mission house and watch the Fijians cutting up human bodies, wrapping the parts in leaves and putting them in the oven. Some of what he saw was so horrendous that he couldn't bring himself to put it in print.

If any of you have read **The Cannibal's Cookbook**, you know that what he did record is horrendous enough. But horrendous as it was, there are things happening on the planet today that make Fijian cannibalism look like a family barbecue. Not only that, I don't even have to look out my window. The stuff is beamed right into my living room. Just like Thomas Williams, daily I see human beings, consuming and being consumed by their fellow human beings. That's how I got the metaphor. As for the title, following my fieldwork, I came home to Vancouver. Soon thereafter, I was introduced to a publisher from Toronto. My friend said, "This is Pamela. She's an anthropologist and has just returned from the Fiji Islands." As a joke the publisher retorted, "Oh, are you going to write 'The Cannibal's Cookbook'!"

It was destiny! And all the parts neatly fell into place. Part I: "Cannibalism Yesterday And Today". About the literal cannibalism of 19th century Fiji—a chilling read—and its use as a metaphor for things happening around the planet today. Part II: "Recipes For Human Sacrifice". Thirty stories about strange and exotic rituals from around the world—literally brought home to reveal how, through our seemingly innocent cultural institutions, we are taking part in the same sacrificial behaviour ourselves.

At the end of each of the thirty "Recipes", there is a short "horrendum" as I like to call it, from the pen of the Rev. Thomas Williams, who, incidentally, eventually gave up trying to convert the Fijians to Christianity. He left the archipelago, went to Australia and became guess what—an anthropologist! Then Part III: "Time To Take Stock". It moves from the specific to the general, from the anecdotal to the analytical to show how culture weaves its spell. We uncover four truths of culture. (I call them my "Four Global Truths".) There's the outward truth, the inward truth, the hidden truth and the forgotten truth. There's a short chapter on each of these in the book, but here they are in a nutshell.

The outward truth: the socially powerful exploiting the exchange system. The history of human society is the history of

Pamela J Peck

a small minority ruling over and exploiting the majority. It has happened in cultures around the planet and across the ages.

Why can they do it? Because of **the inward truth—** people are in love with their chains. You could never have enough police, enough military to enforce the inequalities. You have to get people to accept their exploitation voluntarily. And how do you do that? As the preeminent sociologist and psychoanalyst Eric Fromm put it, "by filling their minds with fiction and distortion, justifying and explaining the minority's rule".

Why would people believe such fiction and distortion? Because of the third truth—and here is where it gets cosmic. It helps us deal with our fate as mortal beings. We are doomed to die and know it. So we create cultural symbols—buildings, monuments, medals, titles—things that do not age or decay—to quiet our fear of our ultimate end. Ernst Becker, in his book **The Denial Of Death**, says that culture is a lie about the possibility of victory over death. I think it's not so much a lie as it is a substitute activity. It's like looking for something in the wrong place. It's **the hidden truth** of culture: the denial of death and its emergence in the form of substitute activities.

The reason I say culture is a substitute activity is because of the fourth truth: **the forgotten truth**. While the hidden truth is about death, the forgotten truth is about life. The reason we strive for immortality, say the sages, is that deep inside we intuit it. To intuit is not to know in the sense of being able to think your way through something, but rather a gut feeling, a kind of deeper knowing that there is something prior.

A state that is One, Whole—that's with a "w"—and Undivided. People who have experienced deep meditation and those who have had a near-death experience talk about this state of blissful Unity. Physicists have talked about it too in terms of the universe not being composed of matter at all but rather of energy and information. The key idea in the forgotten truth is that until we awaken to that Unity, we will remain spellbound in our separateness.

That's Part III of the book. Now, once we've uncovered how culture weaves its spell, then we are in a position to release its hold on us. And that's what Part IV is about. It's called "Entertaining Ideas" and it's a step-by-step process for collapsing the progressive layers of artificial boundaries that keep us locked inside our separateness—from persona to ego to centaur, all the way to impermanence itself. Each of these four has a short chapter as well. In the process, we shatter the illusion of the culturally constructed separate self.

It's not that there is something to be done; there is something to be seen—and seen through. Like seeing through a magic trick. The magician holds us in his power because we don't know where to look. If we were to shift the direction of our look and see his slight of hand, the illusion would have no more power over us. That's at one level. But at the deeper psychological level, we don't want to look. We don't want the spell to be broken. We have paid to see the illusion and we are willing to "pay the price".

It's the same with culture. We don't know where to look—and at a deeper psychological level, we don't want to.

We want to live with our illusions and we are willing to pay the price. So culture, like the magician, does what it does best: it allows us to deceive ourselves.

Finally, there's Part V: "The Dinner Party" which offers some simple "Table Manners". Metaphors again. "Pass the food around; there's plenty." "Don't take more than your share . . .." Basic things like that, and the book ends by "Saying Grace".

So will life be a dinner party or a cannibal feed? Will we feast with or on each other? Toast the abundance or carve up the spoils of the kill? If we don't decide what we want for our lives and what kind of planet we want to leave our children, the cultural forces will decide for us. It's called human history—and it's got us booked for lunch! It may be our fate as social beings—but it need not be our destiny as human beings.

ONE STEP FORWARD, TWO STEPS BACK

Talk Given to the Council of Canadians
West Vancouver, 1996.

I want to thank you for inviting me here tonight to address a timely Canadian issue. It seems our beloved Canada is having a unity problem. And I say 'seems' because, as we shall see, appearance is everything and often has little to do with reality.

I'm going to go about this in a rather oblique fashion, so two things to clear up before we start. First, what I say at the outset may not appear to be connected to the topic. But it is. In fact, I'm not even going to begin in Canada. I'm going to do something anthropological and go to another location and culture. And the reason I'm doing that is because it is difficult to see something when you are inside it. Sometimes you have to step outside, and look in from out there. That's what I do in **The Cannibal's Cookbook**. I take people to faraway cultures to witness strange and exotic rituals, then show them from that outside perspective that we are doing the same bizarre things right here at home.

Second, it may appear that I am making light of a very serious issue. I have reasons for doing it this way. First, the Canadian unity issue has become very heavy and I think we need to lighten up a bit. And secondly, sometimes we have to make light in order to see the light.

I invite you now to sit back and armchair travel with me as we do a little walkabout Down Under—or "Down Unda" as the Aussies would say. We have here a sort of map of Australia, showing the state lines of New South Wales, Queensland, Victoria—British colonialism is evident, isn't it. Then there's South Australia, Western Australia and the Northern Territory, as well as some islands off the coasts. And I've marked a few of the major centres: Sydney, Melbourne, Adelaide, Perth and Brisbane.

If you want to travel to Australia, you might like to get there on Australia's international airline. Do you know the name of it? "Quantas", I hear you say. Let me write down what I think you have answered: Q-U-A-N-T-A-S.

Does that look right? Yes? Okay, does anyone know what it means? No? Does it mean anything? No, Quantas doesn't mean anything. It's not even a word. What's more, it's not the name of Australia's international airline. The word is "Qantas" and it is spelled Q-A-N-T-A-S. The reason we hear it as "Quantas" and write it Q-U-A-N-T-A-S is because our brains are programmed to hear and see the letter "u" after the letter "q". Interesting, eh! And what does "Qantas" stand for? It's an acronym for "Queensland and Northern Territory Air Service". A small bunch of bush pilots.

Where did Qantas fly? Principally out of Brisbane (here on the map) to two major centres in the north. To Darwin, capital of the Northern Territories and to the town of Cairns in northern Queensland. Over time the routes spread within and beyond the national boundaries and QANTAS eventually became Australia's international flagship. Simply put, over time, one component—in the eastern and northern part of the country—came to speak for the country as a whole.

Now let's look at those two locations in the north: Darwin and Cairns. Do you see how they are spelled? D-A-R-W-I-N and C-A-I-R-N-S. We pronounce them "Darwin" and "Cairns". But the Aussies pronounce them "Da-win" and "Cains". In other words, they leave out the letter "r". It's in there, but it's as though it's not there. In other words, their brains are programmed not to see or hear the letter "r".

Now, in the Land of Oz, we have uncovered some very interesting phenomena. If we are conditioned to believe something does exist, we will see it even though it is not there: (the "u" in QANTAS). Conversely, if we are conditioned to believe something does not exist, we will not see it even if it is there: (the "r" in Darwin and Cairns). Further, in the course of history, a part can come to speak for the whole: (QANTAS as synonymous with Australia at large). Please keep those phenomena in mind.

Now lets go to Canada. Another crude map, this time marking the boundaries of ten provinces (notwithstanding the northern territories and some islands off the coasts). And one of those provinces, a distinct society, does not fit in the country. Which one is it?

Let's see. We start with Upper and Lower Canada. They're in. Were from the beginning. Then there's the "New" provinces: New Brunswick, New Scotland. Newfoundland too—and more on that later. I happen to come from New Scotland; you probably know it as Nova Scotia. The reason we say it in Latin is to boost our self-esteem.

British colonialism is evident, isn't it! Brunswick, Scotland . . . even more so with Prince Edward Island, Alberta (named after Prince Albert), and British Columbia. Just like in Australia, so no confusion there.

That leaves Saskatchewan and Manitoba. Now Manitoba sits in the centre of Canada; it's the very heart of the country. And let me say that Manitobans—along with the people of Newfoundland—are as Canadian as you can get. Because they alone have mastered the unique art of Canadian politics; which is, simply put, saying no to yes. Remember, it was a Manitoban, with Newfoundland support, who defeated the Meech Lake Accord. And it was a Newfoundlander, with Manitoban support, who kick-started the big Canadian unity rally a year ago in Montreal. Why do I say "with Manitoban support'? Because—and this is a little known fact—the Manitobans follow, indeed, are named after none other than Mr. Canada himself—from Newfoundland—the man Brian Tobin. Manitobins! See, nobody knows this.

That leaves Saskatchewan. Truly, the odd province out, a province like none other in the country. They even make jokes about it and that's a sure sign that it's different from the others. You've probably heard the one about the American couple who is traveling in Saskatchewan and gets lost. They go to a gas station and the husband asks the attendant, "Can you please tell us where we are?". No, wait a minute, they wouldn't have said "please", so let me set that up again. They go to a gas station and the husband asks the attendant, "Can you tell us where we are?" to which the attendant replies, "Saskatoon, Saskatchewan". The distraught American turns to his wife and exclaims, "Good Lord, Mabel, they don't even speak English here!"

Once back in the fifties, when I was traveling with my family by car through the southern United States—and this is a true story—we stopped at a gas station. The attendant saw our Nova Scotia license plate and said to my Dad, "Nova Scotia. Where is that?" to which my Dad replied, "In Canada." "Canada," the attendant replied, "Is that anywhere near Saskataani?" The guy was confused. Saskataani is not the name of the province. It's the name of the people.

And these Saskataanis are truly inventive. They have to be because they live in the only truly landlocked province in Canada. Every other province—except Alberta— has ocean on its doorstep, and Alberta has major rivers running into the ocean. Poor Saskatchewan, "a river runs through it".

But not to be undone: what they lack in water, they've got in wheat. They've got oceans of it and if you go there, especially in the late summer, you can see waves made of wheat. They're swimming in wheat. So what did they do? They made a Saskatchewan Wheat Pool.

They're inventive in other ways as well. Like they don't waste a lot of time doing routine household chores. In the other provinces, for example, we mow our grass every week or so.

The Saskataanis mow theirs only once a year. And have you seen the size of their lawn mowers!

They don't mince words either. They speak "Canadian, eh" with great economy. Like, for example, here in Vancouver we have many words to describe our winter weather: overcast, rain, showers, drizzle, cloudy, humid, sultry. In Saskatchewan, they use only one word to describe theirs: cold!

Yes, they've had a really rough ride of it. They've got Stampeders coming at them from the west and Blue Bombers from the east. And they know it. They even refer to themselves as the Saskatchewan Roughriders. They're good sports.

There they sit, like a land bridge, keeping the two ends of the country together. Take Saskatchewan out of Canada and there would be a big hole in the middle of it. Think of it: two provinces sitting on one side, with some islands off the coast, and the rest of Canada sitting on the other. Not only that, they're Canada's breadbasket; we need them in the country.

Not to worry. Why? Because they don't know they're a distinct society. Remember, if we are conditioned to believe something does not exist, we will not see it even if it is there. But remember the corollary too. If we are conditioned to believe something does exist, we will see it even though it is not there. And Canada, being the funny kind of country that it is, we've got one of these provinces too. You know it, "la belle province"! Quebec: home of Canada's national anthem—"O Canada", home of Canada's national emblem—the red maple leaf, and home of Canada's national drink—maple syrup. Saskatchewan doesn't even have any red maple trees.

Here's the question: How does a perceived difference in Lower Canada come to speak for the country as a whole? It isn't lower, by the way. Quebec has Mont Tremblant, Mont Sainte-Anne and Mont Sainte-Marie. It's Saskatchewan that's "lower"; the highest elevation is only a hill.

So why do we think we have a unity crisis? Well, let's go back to the beginning. A big bang, a big ball of rock, a big chunk of ice and a meltdown. People start migrating. Here they come: Micmacs, Cree, Algonquins, Plains Indians, inland Salish, Haida, Tsimshian . . . a host of people from God knows where making up the first stage of our cultural history: a land of "First Nations".

The Natives get things rolling and then what happens? The neighbours arrive. Not their neighbours, mind you. Those European neighbours, the English and the French. The ones who aren't getting along at home in Europe—and they don't get on any better here. Squabbles aside, the really astonishing thing is that neither of these neighbours seems to notice that by the time they get here, the land is already taken. Never mind, they just stake out their territory—unfortunately, the same territory—and, confounding all logic, set up stakes as uneasy neighbours again. Now Canada moves from being a land of First Nations to its second stage of cultural history: a land of "Two Solitudes".

Of course, there is work to be done. More than they can or at least want to do. So they open the doors and people flow in from everywhere: from Italy and China, from Greece and India, from Russia and Ukraine. They give some of these new immigrants land to settle on. Not their land in Upper and Lower Canada, mind you. No, they give them land out in Saskatchewan!

Oh, Canada: one big national dream, stretching from sea to sea to sea to "see all that water they've got up there". So they build a railroad to connect it—the CPR—followed by another railroad—the CNR—to keep it safe from the "see all the water they've got up there". Now Canada moves from being a land of "Two Solitudes" to its third stage of cultural history: a land of "Cultural Mosaic".

Now, the thing about a mosaic is that the tiles have well defined edges. Each tile in a mosaic is clearly distinct and separate from every other. Canada: a collection of distinct societies—and we in Canada have prided ourselves on this cultural mosaic, ranking it superior to the melting pot approach of "see all that water . . .." The Americans seem to like it too. Some of them immigrate right alongside the Czechs and the Portuguese, the Iranians and the Japanese.

And then the pivotal event starts to happen. We don't see it—in part because we aren't expecting to see it—but also because we're looking somewhere else. We've got our eyes trained on the outgoing CPR and CNR, and in rolls the CSR: the California Sushi Roll.

Do you see what is starting to happen? A touch of Japan, a touch of America, blended together to create something distinctly different within Canada. The sharp edges of the tiles gradually give way and begin to blend with one another. Thai pizza . . . tofu burgers . . . spaghetti with clam sauce . . . separate cultural patterns from all over the world interweaving with each other, thereby transforming Canada to a fourth stage of culture history, from a land of "Cultural Mosaic" to a land of

"Canadian Tapestry".

The politicians haven't noticed this one step forward. They're busy looking two steps back, still trying to deal with the Two Solitudes, while Canadians across this great land are no longer content to be hyphenated peoples: Indo-Canadians, Punjabi-Canadians, Chinese-Canadians, Japanese-Canadians. No! Canadian Canadians! Distinct Canadians!

So Canada as "Two Solitudes"? English Canadians and French Canadians? No, a "Canadian Tapestry", a new society, a rich blend of colour and shape and dimension; in short, Canada as a model for the 21st century.

Remember: if we are conditioned to believe something does exist, we will see it even though it is not there: "Two Solitudes", Quebec separation, a crisis of national unity, the breakup of Canada . . .. And if we are conditioned to believe something does not exist, we will not see it even if it is there: a "Canadian Tapestry", the creation of a new society, Canada as a model for the 21st century . . ..

Which will it be? See what is not there and not see what is there? Or see what is there and not see what is not there? Will we all speak together and move Canada one step forward—or let the part speak for the whole and retreat two steps back?

A WONDERFUL LIFE

Commentary written on New Year's Day
Vancouver, 1997

As we usher in a new year, we are usually moved to make resolutions. This year, I feel led to make predictions—not for myself but for Canada. My predictions are shaped by two recent artistic anniversaries and a hostage taking—three events that at first sight would appear to be totally unrelated.

1996 marked the tenth anniversary of the smash musical hit, **Les Miserables**, based on Victor Hugo's classic novel, which painfully reveals the squalid conditions of the French underclass. "Do you hear the people sing, singing the song of angry men," declare the lyrics. "It is the music of a people who will not be slaves again . . .." The song is by and for people who have reached their breaking point—when distribution of wealth and opportunity has become so inequitable that it is no longer bearable.

1996 also marked the fiftieth anniversary of that classic Christmas film, **It's a Wonderful Life**, with the now familiar figure of George Bailey who gets a chance to see what life would be like in his home town of Bedford Falls had he not been born.

Simply put, there would not be a Bedford Falls. Without George—played by James Stewart—the town is renamed for the mean and miserly Mr. Potter who controls the commerce, hence, the lives of the people. The point of the film is that no life can be measured a failure, regardless of shattered and broken dreams, where one engages in even seemingly insignificant acts of human kindness. It's a poignant reminder of how many lives can be altered—even destroyed—by the forces of greed without our vigilant intervention.

There is a deeper lesson in the film for Canadians, I believe, because in that same half century we have managed to transform our beloved country from a Bedford Falls into a Pottersville, where banks make blasphemous profits while unemployment tops the list of year-end concerns for Canadians. It is reflective of that disturbing scene of glitzy, money-hungry Main Street, Pottersville, right down to the grotesque appearance of government-operated gambling outlets popping up in bars, restaurants and corner stores across the land. Governments become addicted to the profits of iniquity—and those who can least afford it fall victim to its glittering temptations.

Down-sizing, government layoffs, job insecurity, the dismantling of the social safety net, line-ups at the food banks, begging in the streets, crime in the suburbs . . .. Canadians are deeply troubled about the future while corporate profits soar through the roof and wealth concentrates in the hands of fewer and fewer people . . .. We are buying into the myth of market-driven globalization while in the process, creating the very conditions that make us slaves to it.

It's nuts! More than that, it's cannibalistic—for what is

cannibalism but human beings, consuming and being consumed by their fellow human beings. Socially and economically speaking, we are devouring each other. We would do well to heed the messages of **Les Miserables** and **It's a Wonderful Life**.

We have just had a real-life reminder of consequences of blatant inequality—the hostage-taking incident involving some of our compatriots (among a few hundred others) inside the Japanese Ambassador's Residence in Lima, Peru. It seems the Ambassador's wine and cheese party was rudely interrupted by "Marxist rebels" who are outraged that Japanese development in Peru is benefiting only those who are already rich. These "guerrillas" would like to negotiate some social and economic reforms. Unskillful and unwise as their action must be judged to be, not to mention its flagrant disregard for human life, it must nevertheless be recognized as a desperate cry for help from people marginalized too far for too long. Something had to give . . ..

It is noteworthy in this context that the hostages complained about lack of air-conditioning and poor sanitary conditions inside those crowded quarters. And rightfully so. But pull back the camera from that expansive ambassadorial residence and give us the wide angle shot: we see sprawling crowded slums that do not appear to have any amenities, let alone air-conditioning and sanitation. And conditions are not likely to improve: no negotiations, asserted the Peruvian President. Indeed, it looks as though all that those otherwise "reasonable people" (as their captors were described by hostages already freed) will get for their brazen effort is loss of their citizenship!

At the end of **It's a Wonderful Life**, when George Bailey is down on his luck, the good people of his hometown rally to help him. Freely handing over their savings, they raise a toast "to the richest man in town," appreciating that their own good fortune is a result of his investment in them. George Bailey ends up rich, not because he played the corporate game and won, but because he put himself on the line for people and stayed the course with them to the finish. His was the triumph of the human spirit in the face of corporate single-mindedness and greed. George Bailey emerges a true hero.

Unfortunately, we don't have a George Bailey. Instead, we have Donovan Bailey, a sprinter who won an Olympic gold medal for Canada in 1996. He's our idea of a hero—the guy who beats everybody else to the finish line. And when someone challenges his right to be called "the fastest man in the world", the good people of his "home town" (Oakville, Ontario) rally to help him, too. Freely handing over their savings, they raise a toast to the fastest man alive. And there the similarities end. The people of Oakville are surrendering their money for an advertising campaign to promote the privileged status of someone who is elsewhere raking in lucrative endorsements from self-serving corporate sponsors. Tragically, it is a fitting metaphor for what is happening to the country as we approach the millennium.

Welcome, Canada, to the club-or-be-clubbed corporate mentality of Pottersville!

NOW THEY KNOW US, EH!

Retrospective on the 2010 Winter Olympics
Vancouver, Canada

The first cheers went up when the long anticipated announcement sounded over the airways from the IOC in Switzerland: "The 2010 Winter Olympic Games have been awarded to the city of . . . Vancouver." Years later, the reality of hosting the 2010 Games "came home" when the Olympic torch arrived on Canadian soil. Excited citizens from coast to coast lined the route to witness and cheer those selected to be torch-bearers as they proudly carried the flame across this vast land, seemingly oblivious to the fact that the Olympic torch relay had its origin in the propaganda machine of Hitler's Nazi Germany. Sometimes it takes the wisdom of a child to return us to our senses. I asked a little seven-year-old girl if she went to see the torch relay when it passed through her hometown in Penticton, B.C.

"No," she replied without hesitation, "It's just a torch. I don't know what the big deal is about."

Well, the big deal, according to those who seemed to be in the know, was that the Games would "put Vancouver on the map". But wait a minute; didn't Expo 86 put Vancouver on the map? Of course, many of those expounding the long-term benefits of the 2010 Games were too young—or perhaps not yet born—when Expo 86 turned Vancouver into a "fair city".

The real "big deal" was, actually, the corporate deal—and it didn't take long to surface. Soon after winning Canada's first gold medal, the beaming athlete posed for the cameras sporting—not his snowboard—but a new Omega watch. A member of Canada's women's hockey team appeared in a McDonald's ad, proclaiming that this is where she goes for breakfast with her parents. Really? But perhaps the winner of the "big deal" was the slogan splashed on the billboard in the hockey arena; it read, "Let them know whose game it is: Coca-Cola". They were telling the truth—unwittingly.

The athletes did not appear to be aware of this Olympic "corp.-deal"; they were distracted by the Olympic "or-deal", the big business of winning competitions, somehow feeling an added pressure to bring home the gold because the Games were on home soil. The Canadian Olympic Committee didn't make it any easier for them; they were to "Own the Podium", and for some who failed in the quest, it was all too much. I watched one young female athlete in tears, distraught that she had let her country down. The personal cost was just too high.

The cost in monetary terms was too high as well: local businesses compromised because of street closures . . . close to one billion dollars for security . . . a hundred thousand tax-payer dollars for tickets for the City of Vancouver . . . one million tax-payer dollars for tickets for the Government of British Columbia . . . an untold amount of tax-payer dollars for tickets for the Government of Canada . . .. Then there was the snow — or, more correctly, the lack of it. They trucked it in at a hefty price, to be covered, the local VANOC spokesperson reassured us, by a healthy contingency fund. When pressed to declare if they might go over-budget, VANOC promised transparency; they would produce all the figures — but only after the Games were over.

Of course, one must not forget that much of the work was done by a very large contingent of volunteers. I met a few of them — like the young woman whose assignment was eleven hours per day for 15 days, standing beneath Cambie Bridge, guarding one of the entrances to the Olympic Village. Another was a not-so-young man volunteering at a Bombardier train station. His assignment was an 8-hour shift for a total of 61 days. "Are there any perks for this volunteer work?" I asked him. "I get to keep the jacket," he replied.

Perhaps I am glossing over the deeper significance of the Games, reminded, as I am, that in their nascent form, the Olympics served as an alternative to local warfare. Perhaps it will help our troops "serving" in Afghanistan; they are watching the Games. But when the cheering is over, they return to the task at hand, one that still includes killing and being killed.

But maybe I'm too jaded. What about the value of the Games in deepening Canadian patriotism? Everyone is talking about patriotism and how our favourable medal showing has boosted it. And now that we have begun paying our athletes when they win medals, might we look forward to becoming even more patriotic? I mean, are we really going to pay our athletes to win medals so that we can feel better about ourselves? And are we going to do it under the guise of patriotism? Is this what patriotism is really about? Waving Canadian flags might be innocent enough, but one must be careful not to mistake patriotism for nationalism. All that show of Canadian team support was more properly a display of nationalistic fervour—and nationalistic fervour can easily get out of hand. On one occasion, in the midst of a sea of flag-waving and cheering Canadian fans, a Vancouver policeman advised an American visitor to put away his American flag "for your own protection".

So what is left? Canadian identity. Perhaps hosting the Games will "tell people who we Canadians are". The symbols and the ceremonies were the primary vehicles to that end. So what did people learn about us and about our country? Well, it would appear that those in charge of the telling were not Canadian, nor were they "at home" with our geography and culture. For a start, they chose the inukshuk—a symbol of Canada's north—as the symbol for Vancouver. I have a hunch the creators were snooping about the city for clues, and saw the six-meter high inukshuk in English Bay, perhaps having been born too distant or too recently to know that it was a gift to the City of Vancouver from the Northwest Territories Pavilion at the close of Expo 86. Had those creators ventured a bit further—like, say, into Stanley Park—they might have discovered the totem poles, the preeminent symbol of the Pacific Northwest. Might not a totem have served as a more appropriate symbol!

And what did the world learn about who we are in the opening and closing ceremonies? Once again, stereotypes and clichés prevailed. We are First Nations people who dance and beat drums. We have moose and we have beavers, not to forget red-coated Royal Canadian Mounted Police. Our cultural icons were amassed and paraded in oversized caricature, a tribute to our ability to make fun of ourselves. "Now you know us, eh!" stated the head of VANOC at the closing ceremony. Yes, now they know us, the people of the great white north who make love in a canoe.

But who are we, really? For we ourselves are the people we are trying to tell who we are! What are our principles? Our values? What is worthy of our patriotism? I remember some years back, watching Canada win gold at another international hockey tournament. When the game ended, I listened from my balcony as the streets of Vancouver erupted with the cheers of exuberant fans and the blowing of horns. I turned back to the television to catch the news, in time to watch an Air Canada jet lifting off the runway after rescuing a planeload of Indo-African refugees from the lunacy and rage of Idi Amin's Uganda. Never have I felt more patriotic, more grateful to be Canadian. This is who we are. Go, Canada, go!

The 2010 Winter Games over, our athletes returned to their home communities sporting their shiny medals, with the press and cheering fans at airports to greet them. Now we know them, eh! Canada's new heroes! At the same time, our Dart team returned home—without fanfare—after what can only be described as a heroic medical response to the earthquake in Haiti. Soon after, another team of Canadians assembled water purifiers and emergency supplies to help in the rescue effort after an earthquake in Chile. Yes, this is who we are. Go, Canada, go!

Having said all that, and principles and values aside, thank goodness one of the players from "our" Olympic men's hockey team won that overtime goal to give Canada that final gold medal! How could we possibly have managed through our Olympic post-partum depression without it! Hockey: it's "our" game—and we let them know whose game it is.

Now they know us, eh!

OWE, CANADA!

A Retrospective from Ottawa on Canada Day, 2010

It's July 1st and I'm on Parliament Hill for the grand celebration. Not the official one this morning, with the carriage bearing the Queen of England and all that codified pomp and ceremony. I watched that part on television in the comfort of my Echo Drive condo overlooking the Rideau Canal.

The Queen said all the right things in her short address: Canada's reputation and important peacekeeping role in the world and all that. Then it was our Prime Minister's turn: he talked about how many gold medals Canada won in the Vancouver Olympics! Really! As though that is what Canada is about. Now they will institutionalize the "Own the Podium" program with millions of real public gold for a few pieces of plated private gold in the hopes of boosting our national ego. How did we get so pathetically off-track!

It's evening now and I'm on the Hill for the concert and the fireworks. The dignitaries are gone and this party is clearly "for the people". They've turned up in large measure, these patriots of Canada. At least I assume they are patriots, until I witness the massive amounts of garbage strewn on the grounds. Imagine expressing love for your country by dumping your garbage in front of your Parliament—and doing so on your nation's birthday at that!

I feel a sense of . . . well, loss. And it's not just because of all the refuse on the outside of the Parliament. Indeed, the garbage that surrounds me now as I gaze up at the Peace Tower on the Centre Block serves as a fitting metaphor for the rubbish and waste that has, in recent years, taken place on the inside of this impressive and inspiring architecture.

What is happening to my country! Why are we moving in directions that are so, well . . . un-Canadian, like using our military assets in belligerence instead of peacekeeping? Sacrificing our troops in a foreign conflict on the pretense of national security when the real reason is Western (read American) control of the oil in the Caspian Sea? Disregarding our responsibility to protect the environment so we can continue to produce and sell "dirty oil" in the tar sands? Closing our eyes to human rights violations in dubious nation states in order to further our interests in foreign trade?

Add to all the above, our reckless government spending: the recent G-20, with its billion dollar price tag—for security alone; the G-8 expenditures, complete with an artificial "lake" as a photo backdrop; a 9-day visit from "Her Majesty" to the tune of one million dollars per day . . ..

This last one remains an inexplicable anachronism. The British monarch says she feels at home here in Canada. I should think so. If someone were to spend a million dollars per day for me to have a nine-day visit to England, I think I would feel at home there too. Come to think of it, I was born "British" and my father traveled on a British passport. Not that either of us was actually born in the British Isles; we both had our birth in the Dominion of Canada. But that was prior to 1946, the year that Prime-Minister Mackenzie King's Liberal government passed the Canadian Citizenship Act, which came into effect on January 1st, 1947, the year King himself became the first Canadian citizen. Like King, my origins are "British", but in spite of it, I bet I could not get British citizenship today!

I don't know why my ancestors left England to come to Canada. I imagine they were hoping for something better that made leaving their native land an easy choice. I may never know the reason, but I am glad that they did, for had I not been born in Canada, I would not have been able to get citizenship here either, for the simple reason that I could not in good faith swear an oath of loyalty to their Queen, Canada's head of state.

A few days have passed now. The Queen is in Toronto in the midst of a heat wave. Never mind, people line the barriers at the provincial legislature, in the hopes of catching a glimpse of "Her Majesty" and a chance to offer her copious bouquets of flowers. Television commentators praise the 84-year-old monarch for her fortitude, and one must acknowledge that she does play her role very well. However, no one comments on the honour guard, dressed in full military attire and sporting rifles, standing there in the heat the whole time the dignitaries move from the comfort of their air-conditioned limousines into the comfort of the air-conditioned legislature before emerging for that long awaited walkabout. There seems to be no limit to the deference, expense and special treatment Canadians are prepared to shower on the British royals. These loyal subjects appear willing and compliant participants in this hypnosis of social conditioning. I wonder if, in their private moments, the British royals ever contemplate how long it will be before their loyal subjects figure it all out and put an end to the whole feudal charade.

Another news bulletin: a tornado has made a direct hit on a "reserve" in northern Manitoba. Much of the community has been leveled, and the estimate of damage is about three million dollars. A CBC television reporter interviews a few First Nations people who have lost everything; they don't know how long it will take to replace their meager belongings.

"O Canada, our home . . . on native land!" I know the Government of Canada cannot come to the rescue of everyone, but our priorities are sadly askew, and especially blatant when it comes to the treatment of the First Nations people who were here long before the British arrived. Here stands Canada, almost 150 years old now, still attempting to govern itself on the vestiges of British feudalism while perched on a "True North" chunk of real estate dominated by American interests to the south.

"O Canada, we stand on guard for thee!" But how do we stand on guard in a labyrinth of institutions based on an anachronistic history and foreign dominated culture? Perhaps we might begin standing on guard by shifting from a Governor-General to a Guardian-General. Perhaps we could change the designation of "Crown land" to "Canada land". Perhaps we could let our Parliament truly parle for the people, and cease to call our governing body a "House of Commons", cognizant that this institution was designed to appease so-called "commoners". Perhaps we could abolish our Senate, recognizing its original purpose as an institution to keep "commoners" in their place, thereby preventing their signing into law anything that might erode the unbridled privileges of rich landowners and titled lords. Perhaps then we might be able to show our "true patriot love" . . . for all the sons—and daughters—of this great land.

"O Canada . . ." the band plays as the Queen stands on a raised platform in front of the Ontario legislature. On this occasion, it is not an anthem but a salute; in other words, it is to be played, not sung. It seems the mayor doesn't know the difference, and he sings the anthem with gusto. "He wasn't supposed to sing," offers the "expert" guest interpreting the ceremony alongside the television commentator. "Everything is codified, down to the smallest detail," he explains.

Yes, everything is codified—and for a convenient reason! It prevents any opportunity to challenge the status quo. The monarch speaks; you answer. The monarch shakes your hand; you do not shake hers . . .. Everything—and everyone—in the "proper" place—with all the military, police and public funds deemed necessary to keep things in line . . ..

While the Queen is in Canada, our current Governor-General has been whisked off with her family on a fast plane to China. We also learn now that we will soon be getting a new G-G. Not a Guardian-General. No, it's another Governor-General—a man this time. In a media statement, the smiling G-G-to-be comments that he has always had a strong sense of service—to family, to community, to country . . .. Well, now he can "serve" at home and abroad funded by Canadian tax dollars. He can reinforce institutionalized inequality by being the stand-in for the British monarch on pompous and codified ceremonial occasions. He can hand out medals and host lavish dinners at public expense . . .. Service . . . with a smile . . ..

Three weeks later, I'm preparing to leave Ottawa. Another news item: Canada is going to spend nineteen billion dollars on new fighter jets. They say it's to protect our national sovereignty. Wouldn't it make more sense to buy a few drones to keep a lookout for foreign interlopers sniffing about in our northern ice-melting waters?

Nineteen billion dollars! That we don't have!

Owe, Canada . . ..

I wonder how those First Nations people are managing up there on that tornado-ravaged "reserve" . . ..

MISSING AND PRESUMED DEAD

Talk delivered at the University of Arizona
Tucson, 2001, following the attack
on the New York World Trade Center

Missing and presumed dead: searching for God amid the rubble. That's what we're doing. September 11th has got us thinking real hard about the big question again. So where is God? More specifically, where was "He" on September 11th when people in New York City and in Washington and across America and around the world were propelled into shock and grief and fear to the point of numbness?

Someone once said that the death of a single child could make the idea of God unacceptable. But 6,000* innocent human beings in one fell blow? And in such an indescribably horrific—not to mention diabolically successful—fashion? If God were unable to stop it, He is incompetent. If He could have stopped it but chose not to, then He is no better than the perpetrators. Yet, it is true that, as a result of September 11th, people immediately reached out for God. Somehow it made sense to do that—an attempt, perhaps, to make sense of the senseless.

Six thousand* innocent human beings. Reduced to numbers, if you can bring yourself to do it, is a six with three zeros. Add another three zero's. Six million. The horrors of the holocaust might be an even more stark challenge to the idea of God. Given its magnitude and terror, one could hardly subscribe to the idea of a God Who manifests Himself in history, let alone claim that you are one of His chosen people.

The story is told of some Jews in Auschwitz who decided to put God on trial. They charged Him with cruelty and betrayal. No excuse could be rendered on his behalf and no argument advanced in His favour. So they found Him guilty of crimes that would presumably call for the death penalty. The Rabbi pronounced the verdict. Then he looked up and announced that the trial was over as it was time for evening prayer.

That is the paradox. A paradox that enters us into an ineffable mystery, a mystery that continually returns us to that all-important question: "Where is God?"

We are dealing here with a question asked primarily of the three monotheistic religions—Judaism, Christianity and Islam. Why? Because these three faiths proclaim revelation; that is to say, a God who manifests Himself in human history. This is not to say that other religions do not subscribe to notions of God; they do. It means rather they do not expect this God to intervene in human affairs. So we are primarily searching in what Karen Armstrong in her book **The History of God** calls the God-religions: Judaism, Christianity and Islam. We'll be referring to other religions—principally Hinduism and Buddhism—as we go along, but the focus remains on the monotheistic three.

But let's not make any assumptions here. A lot has happened to a Western God since the appearance of the monotheistic three. Fast forward to the 19th century. One major philosopher after another rose to challenge the traditional view of God, at least the God who prevailed in the West. They were particularly offended by the notion of a supernatural deity "out there" which had an objective existence. Hegel was one of them. He substituted the idea of a "Spirit" which was the life force of the world. But the Spirit was dependent upon the world and upon human beings for its fulfillment.

Then there was Nietzsche who proclaimed that God was dead. Nietzsche argued that Science had made notions of God and a literal understanding of creation an impossibility. So he killed God. I once saw a two-frame cartoon about this. In the first frame, a sign read, "God is dead" and was signed "Nietzsche". In the second frame, the sign read, "Nietzsche is dead" and was signed "God". Whatever the case, as of September 11th, God shares something in common with Osama bin Laden: He is wanted—dead or alive.

In Psychology, Freud regarded belief in God as an illusion that mature men and women should lay aside. A personal God was nothing more than an exalted father figure, Freud argued. But he wisely saw that any enforced repression of religion could only be destructive. Like sexuality, he felt, religion is a human need.

Following Freud, the Positivists—those of a rational bent who argue the proof is in the pudding—believed that religious belief represented an immaturity which science would overcome. But science, of course, can only explain the world of physical nature. And science is of little help when a bunch of terrorists hijack a jumbo jet and plough it into a skyscraper—on purpose. So we are back to searching for God amid the rubble. And the God we know is probably some version of the monotheistic One of Judaism or Christianity or Islam. So let's now take a surface look at these three traditions. Don't try to analyze anything at this point. We'll do that later. Right now, if you can, settle into a reflective or meditative frame of mind, and just let yourself get it at the level that you get it. I'm telling you this for a reason that will become clear in a moment.

Judaism, Christianity, Islam. Three great monotheistic religions that originated in the Middle East and which are branches of the same tree. That there is tension among the believers of these three faiths is somewhat of a paradox. For no tree would be so foolish as to allow its branches to fight among themselves. To get beyond the tension, we must go from the branches down deep into the roots. For in those roots, there is a perennial wisdom shared by all three.

Judaism is the first of the three great monotheistic religions that originated in the Middle East. The Torah—the Jewish name for the Pentateuch or the first five books of the Old Testament of the Bible—tells the story of the world from creation up to the Israelite conquest of Canaan. It roughly spans the 20th to the 12th centuries BCE. Each part of the narrative is full of information about the peoples of the country, then called Canaan, their beliefs, customs, conflicts and ambitions. It names the pre-Israelite tribes that lived here as far back as the late Stone Age. It describes in detail the life styles and relationships, world-view and codes of behaviour of these pastoral nomads. It names the places where Abraham and the patriarchs pitched their tents and built their shrines to the invisible gods—places that are called by the same name to this day.

Around 1700 BCE, many of these Habiru—ancient Hebrew people—made their way to Egypt. The Old Testament describes their ordeals as an enslaved people and gives an account of the Exodus, how Moses led them across the Red Sea about 1250 BCE. In their wanderings, these Israelites, as they would come to be known, paused at Mount Sinai, where monotheism was born and Jewish law appeared in the form of the Ten Commandments.

> And God spoke these words, saying: "I am the Lord your God, who brought you out of the land of Egypt.
> You shall have no other gods before me. You shall not make for yourself a carved image or any likeness of me.
> You shall not take the name of the Lord your God in vain.
> Remember the Sabbath day, to keep it holy.
> Honour your father and your mother.
> You shall not murder.
> You shall not commit adultery.
> You shall not steal.
> You shall not bear false witness against your neighbour.
> You shall not covet your neighbour's house, nor anything that belongs to him."

And after 40 years of wandering in the wilderness, the Hebrew people make their way home to Palestine, their land of milk and honey.

In Palestine, the second of the great monotheistic religions was born. Christianity gives us the New Testament, including the four Gospels, the Acts of the Apostles, and Paul's letters to the early Christians, giving them guidelines in their new faith, and encouraging them in the face of persecution. Above all, the New Testament is a record of the life and teachings of Jesus, from his birth in Bethlehem, to his ascension: his preaching as a rabbi, his working of miracles, and the calling forth of his disciples from among the fishermen beside the Sea of Galilee. "Come, put down your nets," he said, "Follow me, and I will make you fishers of men."

One of his most eloquent teachings, recorded in the gospel of Matthew, is the Sermon on the Mount.

> And seeing the multitudes, he went up on a mountain, and when he was seated, his disciples came to him. Then he opened his mouth and taught them, saying:
> Blessed are the poor in spirit, for theirs is the kingdom of heaven.
> Blessed are those who mourn, for they shall be comforted.
> Blessed are the meek, for they shall inherit the earth.
> Blessed are those who hunger and thirst after righteousness, for they shall be filled.
> Blessed are the merciful, for they shall obtain mercy.
> Blessed are the pure in heart, for they shall see God.
> Blessed are the peacemakers, for they shall be called the children of God.

And he taught them how to pray. "Our Father, Who art in heaven . . ."

Prayer: also an important part of Islam, the third of the great monotheistic religions that originated in the Middle East. Islam places itself firmly in the tradition begun by Judaism and Christianity.

Islam was revealed to the prophet Mohammed, who was a merchant from the city of Mecca in what is now Saudi Arabia, in the 7th Century CE. Mohammed is seen as the last in a series of prophets sent by God to earth. The first prophet was Abraham, who is seen as the first Muslim. Other prophets are Noah, Moses, Solomon, Job, John the Baptist, even Jesus, whose messages, for whatever reason, had been lost or corrupted over the centuries. Mohammed was sent to revive and refine the words of these earlier prophets.

The main source of Islam is the Koran—the revelation Mohammed received during his lifetime, and a record of his own life. Muslims regard the Koran (which means "recitation") to be the word of God, as revealed through Mohammed, from 610 CE, when he was 40, until his death in 632.

The Koran is divided into 110 chapters called "suras". The first sura is a prayer, which Muslims frequently quote.

> Praise be to God, Lord of the Universe, the Compassionate,
> the Merciful, King of the day of judgment.
> We worship you and seek your aid.
> Guide us on the straight path,
> the path of those on whom you have bestowed your grace;
> not the path of those who incur your anger,
> nor of those who go astray.

Drawn from the Koran are the five pillars of Islam, outlining the basic religious duties every Muslim must perform. SHAHADA: the declaration of faith. "There is no God but Allah, and Mohammed is his prophet." SALAT: the five daily prayers. Since the day begins at sunset, the five times are sunset, evening, dawn, midday, and afternoon. The faithful are summoned to prayer by the muezzin, whose voice echoes forth from the minaret: "Allahu akbar, ('God is great'). There is no God but Allah. Mohammed is his prophet. Come to prayer. Come to salvation. Allahu akbar." ZAKAT: the payment of alms. All Muslims who are able to do so, should pay one-tenth of their own wealth for purposes laid down in the Koran: for the poor, for those whose hearts need to be reconciled, for those who are burdened with debts, for travelers, for the cause of God. SAWM: fasting in the month of Ramadan. Ramadan is the 9th month of the Muslim year, the time when Mohammed received his first revelation. It is a Holy month, during which all Muslims must fast from sunrise to sunset each day. HAJJ: pilgrimage to Mecca, a sacred place where the central feature is the Kaaba, a 15-meter high stone cube, inset with a smaller holy black stone. Every Muslim who has means must make the pilgrimage to Mecca at least once in his lifetime.

Now you probably responded to one of these three traditions more than the other two, and to a particular aspect of that one: maybe the historical, or the ideas or perhaps a prayer. And your understanding or appreciation of that response is probably different now than when you were a child.

You are not alone. For each of these groups, there is a consensus about God—who He is, what He is like, and what He expects of those who believe in Him. And the idea of God for one group may be meaningless or irrelevant for another.

But that's only half of it. Within each group, the idea of God has yielded a different consensus at different periods of time. This monotheistic God is a historical creature in that He keeps changing! The idea for one group or time may be meaningless to another. Put another way, there is no one unchanging idea or meaning contained in the word "God". Some meanings are contradictory, even mutually exclusive. So the notion of God is flexible. If this were not the case, it probably would not have survived. To make sense of this relativity, we must look at the way men and women have perceived this monotheistic God from the beginning to the present day.

So let's begin at the beginning. Before there was monotheism, it seems there was probably polytheism and before that, as best we can ascertain, anthropologically speaking, animism and animatism. The idea is not so much that "spirit matters", but that, in practical terms, "matter spirits". It is a pragmatic arrangement. And in the earliest known human societies, it probably took the form of what we can best characterize as magical. One of the earliest known forms of art, for example, is that of vivid cave paintings of animals and hunting scenes, suggesting a magical attempt to influence the procurement of food. The idea is that through magical ritual activity, you can manipulate the outside world —make it rain, assure a successful hunt, cause or cure an illness.

Did you hear that? Cause or cure! Magic can also be malevolent—so called black magic designed to hurt or destroy an enemy. But in its positive form, it is well intentioned, practiced to benefit an individual or a group. Please keep that in mind.

As societies moved from hunting and gathering to agriculture, settled communities and food storage made possible villages, then towns, then cities and city-states. The ritual activities of these early civilizations proceeded from magical manipulation to supplication (plea) through prayer and sacrifice to a pantheon of gods or, in our three cases, eventually a monotheistic god. That's a second stage. And some might say this change represents a shift from magic to religion proper. But, as we shall see, this is not quite correct.

And then comes—after a long pause—the age of science. Rational thought will now prevail and that which cannot be proved by reason and inquiry will be relegated to the past. Some would say that religion has no place in this scientific world and that humankind has now reached the pinnacle of the evolutionary process. They would say that humans have shifted from magic to religion to science.

But this labeling is not accurate—for two reasons. First, we have not shifted from magic to religion to science. Rather, what we have done is shift from the magical to the mythical to the rational. What do I mean by mythical? Relative truth as perceived through creative imagination.

Many people might get upset at the suggestion that God is in some profound sense a product of the imagination. Yet it should be obvious that the imagination is the chief religious faculty. It has been defined by Jean-Paul Sartre as "the ability to think of what is not". As far as we know, human beings are the only creatures that have the capacity to do that. The imagination has been the cause of our major achievements in science and technology as well as in art and religion. The idea of God, however it is defined, is perhaps the prime example of an absent reality, which has continued to inspire men and women for thousands of years. The only way we can conceive of God, who remains imperceptible to the senses as to logical proof, is by means of symbols, which is the chief function of the imaginative mind to interpret. If people say, "It's all in your head", you might respond by saying, "Yeah, where else would it be!" Actually, it's in every cell of the body.

So instead of magic to religion to science, we have a shift from the magical to the mythical to the rational. Religion no longer shows up as a stage. In other words, magic and science do not oppose religion. It's all religion; it just shows up in different forms at different times. The very act of deeming religion irrelevant creates Rationality as our new religion.

Put another way, religion is not a stage we go through but rather the stage on which we go through whatever we are going through. For what is religion? A system of beliefs and practices directed toward the ultimate concern of human beings. Who am I? Why was I born? What happens to me when I die? And the answers to these questions change with people and with time.

That's the first reason the "magic/religion/science" labels don't work. Here's the second one. Being able to figure things out—in other words, rationality—does not crown the human evolutionary process. In fact, it marks only the halfway point in our development. There are three very general post-rational stages we can include in our search for the missing God. And this is where things can go in one of two directions —forward or back. If forward, we shall discover the shared brilliance and possibility of Judaism, Christianity and Islam. If we go back, we run into something that can get really dire. And on September 11th, we got a taste—actually a mouthful—of that something really dire.

Let's take a look. Forward first.

The first of the three post-rational stages is what, in metaphysical circles, has been called the psychic or intuitive. It is a stage where people are guided through hunches or gut feelings, and where things seem to happen through chance or coincidence, rather than conscious planning. The process is more accurately described as synchronicity. **Synchronicity**: (def) "the coincidence of events that seem related but are not obviously caused one by the other". And whereas rational thought proceeds from the logic of "if A, then B", psychic or intuitive thought arises from a direct connection between A and B, a kind of deeper knowing, unexplainable in rational terms.

Here's an example. The Swiss psychoanalyst Carl Jung, who probed into the deep recesses of the mind, was treating a deeply troubled American patient in Zurich who later returned home still very depressed. One night Jung awakened suddenly from sleep with a deep pain in the side of his head. He found out later that his former patient—a continent away—had shot himself in the head at that very moment.

On a more positive note, the marvelous creations of music—from the word "muse"—are sometimes attributed to this stage. It is also the stage of manifesting desires as opposed to achieving goals through long and arduous work. We hear more about this stage today because of the influence of eastern meditative practices as well as familiarity with the work of truly intuitive individuals.

Moses, Jesus, Mohammed . . . they intuited an experience of a supreme Being—God, if you like—that could not be knowable through reason alone. Think of it: Jewish law in the form of the Ten Commandments, Christian guidelines in the form of the Sermon on the Mount and Muslim directives in the form of the Pillars of Islam . . . these advanced ideas were not the product of mere rational thought. These "wise guys" were tuning into something much deeper.

Let's move on. Beyond the psychic or intuitive, is the stage described in religious and metaphysical circles as the subtle. This stage is sometimes referred to as cosmic consciousness or God consciousness. In contrast to the creating and manifesting attributes of the psychic or intuitive, this stage is about unexplainable events. We sometimes refer to them as miracles. The subtle experience has been introduced to us as a possibility by these same historical and religious figures—Moses, and his notion of God speaking to him through, as he experiences it, a burning bush; Jesus, healing the lepers and restoring sight to the blind; and for Mohammed, the divine revelation of the

Koran: "Recite!" the angel tells him, a total of three times. Today, Jewish, Christian and Islamic mystics alike attest to the possibility of ordinary human beings entering into this deeper state of consciousness.

And there is one further stage, that which is described in metaphysical circles as the causal. Here all dualities are overcome. There is no A, no B, just timeless, spaceless being. The illusion of the separate ego is dissolved as the individual personality disappears. The causal stage is also known as Unity consciousness. It goes beyond the miraculous as the individual body and the cosmic body are experienced as One and the same. Some refer to it as the Godhead.

When Moses asked the figure in the burning bush whom he should say sent him, the answer came, "'I am that I am. Tell them that 'I am' sent you." Think of God that way. Then think of yourself that way. I am. They are one and the same. No predicate—just I am. No boundary, no separation from another human being or the external environment . . . Unity consciousness. When Jesus was asked about his relationship with God, he answered, "I and the Father are One." They are one and the same. Unity consciousness. And God revealed to Mohammed his timeless word, which took the form of the Koran. It was an epiphany. The mind of Mohammed and the mind of God: they are one and the same. Again, Unity consciousness.

So let's sum up to this point. Magical, mythical, rational, psychic, subtle, causal—in very general terms, these are the stages through which the human species has the capacity to evolve. And the idea is that as we move from magical to mythical or from rational to psychic, for example, we do not reject the earlier form but rather incorporate it at a more enlightened level and move on so that we become more complete, more integrated, more an expression of that Unity which is the universe.

Magical: engaging the universal energy to manifest. Mythical: expressing the mystery to appreciate. Rational: using our God-given intellect to create. We are expanding! So far so good! But if we are not expanding we are diminishing. It's one or the other because we cannot stand still. When we are expanding we are progressing from ego toward higher states of consciousness, the final point being the Unity consciousness of the causal stage. From rational . . . to psychic . . . to subtle . . . to causal.

But what happens, in spiritual terms, if we are threatened by the rational? What happens when we read the scriptures literally and cannot reconcile religious tradition with rational thought? Or when we interpret spiritual concepts as matters that bear their own inherent proof? Well, we regress rather than progress. Instead of moving forward from rational to intuitive, we move backward from rational to mythical. But with a difference, because "mythical" now becomes over-laden with narrow tribal associations. "I am" becomes predicated with the name of the tribe.

The problem is this: in psychological terms, defining oneself as anything less than Unity consciousness represents a split of the rational ego into two conflicting segments—persona and shadow. Persona is that culturally prescribed person we take ourselves to be. It is how we define ourselves as members of the tribe: we are Protestant or Catholic, Jewish or Christian or Muslim . . .. It goes on and on.

One of the results of this cultural role-playing is a deep sense of separation from the outside world, a world that is perceived as hostile and threatening. When we, as individuals, are stuck in the persona, we buy into the hostility while denying that the tendency resides within ourselves. In other words, the tendency does not disappear, we just deny that we have it and locate its source in someone or something else. "Look at what they are doing to us!"

And that which is projected outside the self becomes the shadow. Because we identify only with the persona, we carry on a battle with the shadow. As the battle rages, the self shrinks smaller and smaller while the non-self looms larger and larger "The world is a dangerous place—and it's getting more dangerous every day." Does any of this sound familiar?

In short, if we live in the persona, we shrink the range of our world to protect our self from imagined threat. Two essential ingredients are at play. First, we feel the lack of this tendency in ourselves, and secondly, it appears to be "out there". In other words, we project our attack outward, and imagine people attacking us. So we attack back!

Put simply, there are two principle emotions—love and fear. If you are expanding your consciousness, you are moving forward toward love; if you are diminishing, you are moving backward into fear. And how does this backward movement show up in God terms? As religious fundamentalism. Let's look again at our monotheistic three.

Judaism: Yahweh started out as a cruel and punishing God in the Old Testament. But He did not remain so. The Israelites transformed Him into a symbol of transcendence and compassion. And the God of the Habiru as "I Am" is a unifying concept. As such, Judaism offers a path to higher consciousness. But the myth of a cruel and punishing God has survived, in some respects, in Judaism, (as well as in Christianity and Islam) to this day. And the idea of a Chosen People can rouse a narrow, tribal theology. Armed with such a tribal theology, Jewish fundamentalists have continued to build and settle in the Occupied Territories of the West Bank. Their avowed intention is to drive out Arab inhabitants, using force if necessary. A backward movement . . ..

Christianity: Jesus, probably an itinerant Jewish rabbi —remember, he was not a Christian—preached a message of compassion, and taught that "God is love". (There are only two choices: God is fear or God is love.) After his death, his followers decided he was divine. This development did not happen immediately. The doctrine that Jesus is God in human form was not finalized until the 4th century. Now, this idea could be interpreted either way: forward—Jesus as Logos, the expression of the very Word of God; or backward—Jesus, the victim of a fearsome God who demands human sacrifice. Christian fundamentalists continue to insist on a literal interpretation of scripture—apparently oblivious to the inconsistencies—and seem to have little regard for the compassion of Christ. They are swift to condemn people they see as "enemies of God" and consider any who are not adherents to the faith in its literal interpretation (including Jews and Muslims) to be destined for hellfire. Tribal theology.

And finally, Islam. In Islam, the existence of God is not in question. (Allah, composed of "al-lah" literally means "the god".) In the Koran, an "unbeliever" is not an atheist in our sense, somebody who does not believe in God, but one who is ungrateful to Him, who can see quite clearly what is owing to God but refuses to honour and thank Him; it represents a stance of perverse ingratitude. And when Muslims greet each other with "Salaam alaykum" ("Peace be with you"), they are reminded of God. The external gesture serves as a means of acquiring "God-consciousness". But like any other faith, Islam can be interpreted in a variety of ways. For example, Islamic fundamentalism has interpreted the texts in a manner that is disastrous for Muslim women and has construed the notion of Jihad as holy war in place of personal struggle. It is a highly political spirituality, literal and intolerant in its vision. Muslim fundamentalists have toppled governments, and assassinated or threatened world leaders. They conduct mass terrorism in the name of Islam, and call on Muslims the world over to engage in Jihad as Holy War.

In all three cases, fundamentalism is actually a retreat from God. To make such historical notions as "Chosen People", "Crusade for Christ" and "Holy War" the focus of religious activity is a backward movement. And when this movement continues to deteriorate, the dualism between persona and shadow is exaggerated and we soon get an all out war between good and evil. It's a fight against the evildoers on the one hand

and the infidels on the other—a refrain that is all too familiar. Each side sees good in itself and evil in the other. By contrast, in the transcendent stages, there is no opposition between good and evil.

The God of Jews, Christians and Muslims got off to a bad start, since the tribal deity Yahweh was murderously partial to his own people. Latter-day crusaders who return to this primitive notion are falling into the same separatist trap, sacrificing unity for the exclusiveness of the tribe. Moreover, they are denying the crucial monotheistic theme: ever since the prophets of Israel reformed the old pagan cult of Yahweh, the God of the monotheists has promoted the ideal of compassion.

Compassion: a particularly difficult virtue. It demands that we go beyond the limitations of our egotism, insecurity and inherited prejudice. But go beyond we must—for the idols of fundamentalism are not good substitutes for God. If we are to create a faith that meets the challenges of September 11th, we must look to the past for both inspiration and warning.

So what idea of God works for you—now? That's the question! The God of the Jews? And, if so, which God of the Jews? Is Yahweh the cruel and violent God of the early Old Testament or a symbol of transcendence and compassion? Is your God incarnate in Jesus and, if so, is Christ a symbol of compassion or the sacrificial victim of a fearsome God? Is He the God of Islam and if so, is Allah exclusive and political or the only true reality? Each generation has to create a post-rational experience of God that works for it. Fundamentalism in all three traditions denies this; it believes all experience God in the same way and for all time.

So let me pose a couple of final questions. If I want to achieve a post-rational experience of God, what should I do? Instead of searching for a God descending from high, should I instead be cultivating a sense of God for myself? Instead of a reality "out there" that I can discover through the process of rational thought, can I experience God as a product of creative imagination like the way poetry and music are inspired?

Instead of God existing in reality, perhaps God is reality, an ineffable reality that is beyond time and beyond change. One, Whole and Undivided. Something to draw from, to connect with, each one of us an aspect of that Whole, like drops of water in a vast ocean. Or as with the Hindu notion of Brahman-Atman: Brahman pervades the world while Atman is found eternally within each one of us. The experience of Brahman or Atman cannot be explained rationally any more than can a piece of music or a poem. And it prevents God from becoming an idol or an exterior reality "out there".

This approach is more akin to mysticism. Instead of seeing God as an objective fact, which can be demonstrated by means of scientific proof, mystics have claimed that it is a subjective experience, mysteriously experienced in the ground of being. Mysticism introduces a calmer spirituality into the religions of God. The process of awakening or illumination is very different from the commanding inspiration of prophecy. It has more in common with the tranquil enlightenment of the Buddha.

It is possible to acquire these mystical attitudes. The methods are known and highly developed, especially in the Eastern traditions of Hinduism and Buddhism. Even if we are incapable of the higher states of consciousness achieved by the mystic, we can at least get past the narrow tribal notion of God and cultivate an attitude of compassion.

It's there to be had in all three of the monotheistic faiths as well as in Eastern religions. Martin Buber had a dynamic vision of Judaism as a spiritual process and a striving for unity. Encounter with a personal God, he felt, took place in our meetings with other human beings when we shift from treating others as objects—what he referred to as an "I/it" relationship—to seeing others as an aspect of the All—an "I/Thou" relationship.

Buber realized the term "God" had been soiled and degraded but he refused to relinquish it. He asked, "Where would I find a word to equal it, to describe the same reality?" But he understood those who chose to reject it, since so many appalling things have been done in God's name.

Jesus did one better. He got past the three-letter word and called God a four-letter word. Simply put, God is love. That statement is both simple and profound. For nothing is sweeter than love, nothing stronger, nothing higher, nothing wider, nothing more pleasant, nothing fuller or better in heaven or in earth. For love is Unity consciousness. And Unity consciousness is . . . well . . . God.

It's there in Islam as well. The Hajj offers each individual Muslim the experience of a personal integration in the context of the ummah—the community—with God at its centre. The rituals of the Hajj may look bizarre to the outsider but they unleash an intense emotional experience and express the communal and personal aspects of Islamic spirituality. As expressed by the Iranian philosopher Ali Shariati (recorded in Karen Armstrong's **A History of God** 1993: 156-7):

> As you circumambulate and move closer to the Kaaba, you feel like a small stream merging with a big river. Carried by a wave you lose touch with the ground. Suddenly, you are floating, carried on by the flood. As you approach the centre, the pressure of the crowd squeezes you so hard that you are given a new life. You are now part of the People; you are now a Man, alive and eternal.... The Kaaba is the world's sun whose face attracts you into its orbit. You have become part of this universal system. Circumambulating around Al-lah, you will soon forget yourself . . .. You have been transformed into a particle that is gradually melting and disappearing. This is absolute love at its peak.

Jews and Christians have similarly emphasized the spirituality of community.

So where was God on September 11th? And how do we find Him in the rubble? Here's the bottom line. The energy of the universe, whatever you choose to call it—Yahweh, God, Allah, Spirit, The Force, Cosmos, Universal Law—is impartial and non-judgmental. In moral terms, it functions somewhat akin to electricity; that is to say, it will equally light a cathedral and a brothel. The energy is there to be harnessed . . . for benefit or ill will. It does not discriminate; it will respond to whatever purpose we choose.

So God was—and is—in the choosing. And what we see going on "out there" is a representation—a playing out—of what is going on in our individual and collective psyches.

The most conscious expression of this choice is love. Anything less is an expression of fear—and fear breeds attack. Every attack is a veiled plea for help. Viewed in this context, September 11th was a plea for help. What shall we choose in our response? The God of fear or the God of love?

*At the time this paper was delivered, casualties were estimated at 6000, a figure later revised to less than half that number.

ABOUT THE AUTHOR

Cultural anthropologist Pamela J Peck is an author, composer, playwright and lecturer whose professional interest is education for a global perspective and the application of social science knowledge to the practical concerns of everyday life. Canadian born, she holds the degrees of Bachelor of Arts in Psychology and Religion (Mt. Allison University), Bachelor and Master of Social Work (UBC), and PhD in Anthropology (UBC). She was a Research Associate at the University of Delhi in India and a Research Fellow at the University of the South Pacific in Fiji.

Pamela has traveled in and studied more than eighty countries around the world, and has lived and worked in a number of them. She uses her cultural experiences to infuse and inform her lectures, commentaries, novels, screenplays and stage musicals. Her writings appeal to people of all ages as she takes us on journeys to the far corners of the outer world, and into the inner recesses of the human mind.